MW00951480

ALCOHC

NUTRITION AND MINDFULNESS

SIMPLE STEPS TO STAY SOBER

Staying sober. What to eat and drink and do now you no longer drink. Nutrition and mindfulness to help you live the life you dreamed of.

Catherine Mason Thomas

Second Edition

Introduction

Hello there. I'm Catherine.

I am a coach, personal trainer and hypnotherapist. I am also alcohol free (AF).

I don't usually introduce myself as AF because it's like saying "I'm gluten free", "Justin Bieber free" or "hot pants free". They are facts about our likes but they don't say much about who we really are.

I am going to show you that through the advice, tools and hints in this book your chances of becoming AF or a minimal drinker, and maintaining that is more than possible. It is an 80% certainty (more about that statistic later).

Why go down this road? Because you get your life back.

Once you stop defining yourself in your head as a drinker, party girl or just, plain alcohol dependent, once you change that habit, you stop being a definition and start to be a whole person. It's a big thing to change an alcohol habit but once you do, other things become far more important. Whether you drink or not is no longer central. Being AF is as interesting an aspect about yourself as being a Belieber, it is just one of your characteristics but what you do instead, is far more interesting.

Alcohol will come to define you if you let it. Being AF, you define yourself and leave alcohol behind.

How great does that sound? It's all true and it is in your grasp. Read on.

But that is down the path, I wrote this book to help you change your habit with alcohol and get healthier and happier in the first six months and then six months to a year.

At the end of the first six months, being happy and healthy is far more than just being AF.

Specifically in relation to alcohol: alcohol free in my book, is a stop on the line but not the destination. The destination is to be the most you or I can be. Taking alcohol out or dialing it down takes the brakes off, so you can reach your potential but there is no personality type or state of being called AF. AF is not job done. You are you, whether you have chosen to obscure it behind alcohol or not. The congratulations come and the self-esteem is earned by being yourself, no alcohol mirrors or curtains to hide behind.

This book helps you to meet your own reflection by taking out whole scale or minimizing the personal detour that is alcohol. So buckle in for the ride, it is worth it.

What's different from the First edition?

Well, the tone of this book.

I have re-written a lot of it, particularly the Nutrition section and this Introduction. My Ten Laws and advice on Morning Rituals, nutrition and supplements are still in. So, the change is mainly to the tone of the talk around the advice. You could say that I have lightened up and regained my sense of humour. I certainly hope so. I have also gained more insight into life beyond becoming AF and it has confirmed for me how much better everything is without a drink in your hand or a hangover to contend with.

That's the difference between the First Edition written at 1 year sober and this Second Edition at 18 months sober.

All good then. Probably.

I think the truth is that, further into sober living and practicing what I preach, life has become lighter no doubt about that, and being alcohol free is no longer such hard work. It's a habit, a lifestyle and simply *"I don't drink"*.

What a massive, massive relief.

I do have moments when I still feel the rush of elation that I have done it. I don't drink.

Do you want to be there too? Can you taste it? Are you on the sober bus already? Do you need a bit of extra motivation or encouragement or help to overcome fear?

This book will help you with getting your mindset straight and your toolbox of things to speed your success, fully stocked. It will take you along the path so you feel the benefits as quickly possible and at the end of six months, you should feel so much better than just AF. It will encourage you on to going for a year AF and I will be cheering you all the way.

Ok, your goal may be not to drink, or it may be to dial down your relationship with alcohol to rebalance your life. You may want a wholescale change or a breather. Whichever it is, the benefits I have found of being alcohol free are wide ranging and many:

- ability to function at all times of day

- freedom from obsessing about what, when and where to drink

- energy freed from obsessing

- better health

- more interesting life

- better relationships with my family

- honest emotions – honestly happy and unhappy and everything in between

- more free time to do interesting and enjoyable things

On the road to change there are and were some negatives: I became and still am much more "gobby". If "gobby" does not translate, it means that I put up with less, settle for less, demand more and am irritated by much. Is that a bad thing? Well, I am hoping that I will settle down a bit but being difficult, I do not intend to apologise for that. Alcohol dumbed me down and shut me up.

I have asked more of the people around me. I am not low maintenance anymore. We have gone though some warfare because the people around me were happy with the way things were. Of course they were. I did it all. I asked little of them because alcohol was my friend. So, I have dug in and re-negotiated my relationships, sometimes in a mature manner, sometimes in a tantrum manner but I am getting the job done and as a result, I feel that I matter more and I am myself, warts and all.

If you did not read the first edition so are coming at this fresh, this book is a "How To" guide to help you stay free of alcohol or on the alcohol moderate path using food and positive emotional practices. It is particularly aimed at the first six months but you can read it in the run up to change or if you are longer on the path and are looking at tuning up your emotional or physical health. I take this from the position of coach or trainer, because those are my skills. So you should definitely feel throughout this book that I am encouraging you, urging you on. You can do it. Go on, try.

That all sounds very hard work but it is not. You get a toolbox of things to try which help you rebalance yourself as you change a major habit – alcohol.

You can try it all: the spaghetti on the wall approach – throw every tool at being AF or moderate, and see what sticks.

You can be more strategic and choose a couple of my laws (there are ten to choose from) and see what difference they make. If those don't feel right, choose a couple more, and so on.

There is no perfection, just go with something from the book and see if it makes a positive difference.

Also, don't expect perfection. I know that in the first three months, and I talk about this in the book, you may find that your diet is laughably unhealthy: tubs of ice cream back to back, biscuits by the packet, Haribo in every coat pocket. The priority is to keep to your commitment to change your relationship with alcohol. Period. Everything else does not matter. I will encourage you to move towards controlling your sugar because it actually helps you with becoming AF. I will talk in the nutrition section of this book about the stark research which shows a correlation between sugar and drinking, sugar and relapse. I will also talk about the importance of eating well to support your mood. You can be strategic with your food and it will directly affect your success in staying away from alcohol and feeling happy.

If in the early months, if there is any capacity to make nutrition choices better, this book will help you. I have included the nutrition section because eating with recovery in mind does actually help you in your primary goal. The nutrition advice will make you feel better, calmer and more energetic. So, whether it is the lack of alcohol or the good eating, you will get a faster upside to help you embed your change.

I explain the structure of the book below but let me finish this intro to the intro with a story:

I remember watching a documentary about happiness where the programme makers had taken three people who all wanted to be happier and they gave them six months to try various ways recommended. The person who made the most impression on me was a woman in her fifties who had never married as she had had an unwell mother. Her mother had died and now this women had found herself alone and resenting all the years she had "wasted". Anyway, of all of the subjects, she did the best. She changed from a somewhat bitter woman into someone who radiated joy. It was amazing. This woman had not changed her circumstances. She was still in middle age, unmarried, childless and going through grief at the loss of her mother. But she has found happiness from re-visioning her life using various techniques like gratitude, connecting with people and experiencing new things.

That is what I wanted for me and I want for you. We can't take time back or do anything differently about our circumstances. The only thing we can do is change our futures and the way we see things. The single biggest change you can make to your life to influence everything else is take alcohol out or cut it right back. I am not over playing this.

This book approaches this subject from an emotional health and a physical health perspective. It is a manual with toolkit that does the following:

- Five Steps to a better emotional life (Chapter 1)

- What food to eat specific to recovery from unhealthy alcohol levels (Chapter 2)

- Creating a Morning Ritual to support your new life (Chapter 3)

- Ten Laws of Sober Resilience (Chapter 4)

- What to Eat to Feel Better (Chapter 5)

- What Supplements to take to Rebuild, Manage your Moods and Minimize Cravings (Chapter 6)

- Food to eat to target Liver Repair and "Love Your Liver" recipes

- Free Book Offers and My Other Books

- Conclusion

I have trodden the path you are walking or standing at the start of, wondering whether to place the first footstep. Let me help. It is my pleasure, believe me.

When I decided to write this book, I had been writing and coaching extensively on human potential. I had become AF and had been amazed at what a difference it had made to my mindset and my ability to achieve things I never thought possible. I think alcohol is a silent killer of human potential.

Above the door to every bar, I think they should add a notice which reads:

Beware. Turn back. Entering here will strip you of creativity, ambition, grit, tenacity, peace and happiness"

That may sound extreme and I know it is but if you want to see what you are really capable of, take a holiday from alcohol and find out. As I said, you can't get your drinking years back but you can reclaim your future years before they go the same way.

Having seen the difference that it made to my life and the people I worked with, I thought *"Why don't I gather in one place all the things that I know of that make the alcohol free path easier to start and a joy to live?"*

I prefer the term "alcohol free" to "stopping drinking" or "giving up alcohol" because being "free" of alcohol is the point. It is an opening up of your life, not a life of abstinence (another loaded word).

Being AF is not a prison sentence, it is a new beginning, a chance to recreate yourself into what you really want to be.

This book is therefore a toolkit of behaviours and habits, what to do, eat and supplement to get and stay alcohol free. The third element of this book is advice on how to build the life you want now you have the space that alcohol took up. It is your coach in book form to help you succeed and exceed your own expectations.

The starting line – your story and my story

You are reading this so I think it is a fair assumption that you are on the starting line or just over it.

I want you to think about your own story but to get to you going: My own story, I will give you this now because I think that positive examples are great for motivation and because my story, in a mundane way, dispels some of the lies told about alcohol reliance and getting free:

I was never on a park bench or drinking in the morning. I held down a top job, hit the gym at 6am and parented my children.

The damage I was doing, in the misguided belief that alcohol was helping me to cope, was to myself. I was running too fast and using alcohol to power me through and avoid the obvious, that I was not happy and I was stuck.

I did not know that at the time but I had more than an inkling that there was more gas in the tank in terms of my life fulfilment, if only I could take alcohol out.

I was not a binge drinker, although you may be. I was just a steady imbiber who used alcohol in almost all evening situations: to pep me up, calm me down, give me "me time", make me sociable, give me energy and help me sleep. And so on and on and on.

I felt bad: low, bored and just marking time. I drank in the evenings as a reward for getting through the day, as a holiday from the stress I felt at my job, at past hurts and at uncertainty that my future could be anything different. Outwardly, everything appeared marvellous but inside I was losing myself and pushing down my feelings of overwhelm. The merry go round of work and family punctuated by attempts at "me-time" where I retreated into a drink.

My world got smaller and I withdrew from connection with people. Part of this was because I was hungover a lot of the time so the energy I had was devoted to functioning, nothing left for a deep, emotional life. I was very tired from working and parenting and I thought that alcohol was powering me through. Nutrition seemed a slow way to get the relief that I perceived that I got from alcohol.

The other part was that I did not want anyone to peek inside how I was truly feeling or I would have had to admit that I was miserable and at my own making. I had got myself into this mess. I felt boxed in by a big job, numerous children and a second marriage that I really wanted to work. When I drank, the effect of alcohol made me feel better for a while. A holiday in my head. The thing is, these effects were really momentary. Maybe three or four drinks and then the depression would descend as I knew I had to get up in the morning and do it all again. I felt like a prisoner, walking the line Johnny Cash-style, day after day.

I am not looking to depress you or get your sympathy, just explain how it was for me so you maybe can resonate with the advice in this book. Doing something else to feel better was my driver and it was my own self that started persuading me to change. I was just tired and bored of the person I had become. I wanted something else, definitely without alcohol but not sure with what else

Situational support then came into play. I moved house and had a third and fourth child (twins). My new house was more remote and I needed to drive, just to get my children to school. A quite reasonable fear was that "the game was up" because the school run in the morning would see me over the legal limit for blood alcohol. This made me wake up.

I also felt a new period of my life was beginning with the house move and my age. I was about to turn 50.

There is lots of research that habit change is most likely around personal milestones – birthdays, weddings, post-holiday, New Year etc.

I also started to want more. This is the element in which alcohol no longer serves you but holds you back.

I had changed my job to have more time at home and I wanted to regain some of my old hobbies, particularly sport, horse riding in my case. Driving to the stables hungover was not great and riding was definitely dangerous. I like to do things well and I was never going to regain my riding prowess and get even better if I was always battling a hangover.

So alcohol, in the classic definition, had come to the point when it made my life and particularly my aspirations, unmanageable. It had to go, I knew that.

You may think it odd that someone in the human potential field, would drink or do anything else that runs counter to health advice. Wouldn't humans be simple if they followed their own advice? Doctors smoke. Judges visit prostitutes. There we are.

So, no rock bottom, no arrest, no divorce, nothing particularly bad happened to spur change. It was more my subconscious starting to chatter at me *"Let's do something different" "Let's make the next decade the best" "Let's get rid of alcohol, it no longer serves you" "Look in the mirror and be proud of what is looking back at you" "Stop killing yourself"*.

That is how I started. It did not happen immediately. I had a few attempts as going alcohol free or cutting down. In my case, alcohol free is where I am happiest and I am clear about that. I am only one drink away from my old life and I don't want that life back. My new one is infinitesimally better.

It probably took me five years from the voice in my head starting to talk to me, to the situational changes which made the choice obvious to the acceptance in my soul that change was now. Things definitely sped up so the last period from serious attempt to getting free was about a year.

The final step onto the alcohol free path did not come on some anointed day. I don't believe there is some perfect goodbye to your old life or necessary rock bottom that has to happen to change. One of the lies we tell ourselves about change, is that we will do it *"next Monday"* or *"after Thanksgiving"* or whatever date in the future sounds "right".

My first day alcohol free was a Sunday: January 11 2015. Not January 1st because I just didn't have the resolve on December 31st. January 11th was the day because I had to drive the children to school the following Monday morning and I caught myself debating whether I could find an excuse to walk them or bus them to school. I caught myself and just thought *"Enough. This is humiliating. What have I become that having a drink is worth all of this coping around it"*.

That was it for me. No more debate. I remember thinking to myself *"Why don't I just stop. No more mental flip flopping. Ok"*.

So don't wait for a special day or even debate it too much, just start.

Your starting line

You start from your own place. It may look like mine or it may look entirely different.

That does not matter. What matters is that you are reading this book and will find help in it to start or really get going.

Your starting point could be desperation or worry about the person you have become or your health. It could be interventions from family or friends who confront you about your drinking. It could be a milestone birthday just gone or approaching: 30, 40, 50 or 60 or even 70 or 80 which, with the time ticking, pushes you to take stock and want a better life. It could be a DUI or custody issues or divorce contributed to by your drinking. It could be something much less spectacular or "rock bottom" like, such as a new relationship, job or new child.

One of the lies told about alcohol issues is that you need to hit "rock bottom" to stop drinking. Nonsense.

If you believe that, that belief does not serve you. It persuades you never to stop as it is fatalistic. Ignore that lie.

I don't believe that alcohol is an elevator that you cannot get off until you reach the bottom floor. You may have mini rock bottoms: events where you catch yourself, like me with the school drop off. That is all helpful. But the important thing is that your own self will be telling you to alter your relationship with alcohol. What is the betting that you are reading this because the voice in your soul is saying – change. No-one would take that bet – it is a cert!

I agree that drinking can be progressive so a moderate drinker becomes a hazardous drinker and that can lead down, down into the abyss of alcoholism. That is because the nature of chemical action on the body is that you build up a tolerance. Where one glass of wine was enough to get you to that happy place, it may take more next time and so on. But that image ignores the power of interruption and disruption.

The majority of people pull back their drinking when they are nowhere near the alcoholic, park bench stereotype. The majority of people go nowhere near a park bench or a treatment programme to dial down their drinking. I went near neither and I am the norm.

You don't even have to call yourself an alcoholic to stop drinking. Read that again. You can stop drinking without having to use the A word. The A word is not a magic ticket to sobriety like the golden ticket in Charlie's chocolate bar.

Most people alter their relationship with alcohol, for worse or for better, based on their situation. I am suggesting that external factors play a major role in our drinking. That is because for most people, external factors influence how we feel. Drinking is an attempt to manage our emotions: to switch off unwanted ones and switch on wanted ones.

Let's take the "for worse" usual situation: So, people start to drink more when their situation needs some relief. Maybe you have a hideous boss, or your marriage is breaking up or you have money troubles or aging parents?

Drinking is a coping mechanism so an attempt to deal with situations which are triggering emotions we want to get away from. Admittedly, it is not a great coping mechanism but at the time, it gives relief so it seems the panacea.

The point is that when the situation changes, so for example, our boss gets reposted (hurrah!), our marriage gets back on track (phew!) or we face down our money troubles and get advice and a budget (a massive relief and step towards growing up, however old you are), the majority of us will pull our drinking back. And we will do this without visiting AA or even calling ourselves alcoholics.

I am not dissing AA and in fact, I talk about the value of connection to communities in my Eighth Law of Sober Resilience later in this book. The point I am making is that deciding to dial down our relationship with alcohol does not have to come with all the paraphernalia of AA, the A word and the sack cloth and ashes that puts so many people off just getting started. There are also other networks other than AA which a take a different approach – less about breaking yourself down to rebuild and more about taking the sober spark inside us and giving it some oxygen. I am saying that you can become AF however you like. There is no one path.

Let me come back to the main point here, drinking is situational so if our situation changes, the majority of us will alter our habits, including drinking. The change of situation gives us the insight, strength and space to make changes. That is a way away from the stereotype of walking into an AA meeting straight from the cells after a DUI or from a custody hearing where we have been stripped of our children with no hope of getting them back unless you complete a twelve step programme.

If you think I am wrong on this, take a look at the data on Vietnam veterans and heroin use. Soldiers during the Vietnam War routinely took heroine and other drugs, way above the national average for drug use in the general population. It was a pretty bad situation they found themselves in. If you believe the theory that addictive behaviours are a one way ticket to misery and eventual ruin and death, all those soldiers would have come back as addicts and been in and out of treatment programmes until they died or stayed in treatment programmes whilst battling the urge to drink for the rest of their lives. Not true. The majority got back, reconnected with their friends and families and did not take their coping behavior, heroin, with them. The situation had changed and their behaviour changed.

So, the good news is that it is not true that once a heavy drinker, always a heavy drinker and habit change will fail.

Now for some of us, when we get to the hazardous stage, which I define as drinking above the healthy limit or when it starts to affect your mental health in terms of mood, motivation or relationships, no alcohol is probably a better route than cutting back but you have to choose your own journey.

It is certainly true that getting to the right path for you may take several attempts: like practicing dunking a basketball in a hoop or the triple salco at the ice rink. You may also try moderation and decide that it is just too complicated. I tried moderation and just found it too stressful and it took up too much space in my brain, like counting points at Weight Watchers. But you have to choose your own path and there is no single right way.

This is the process, however hard it is on your self-esteem, as you perceive each "attempt" as a failure. Reframe that: each attempt is feedback on what will make you a success in getting out of an unhealthy relationship with alcohol.

When Michael Jordan missed the hoop, did he give up and say it would never happen. Of course not. So accept failure as feedback and know that you will succeed, particularly if you have chosen or had visited upon you situational changes which make alcohol dominance in your life, unworkable. That is not going away so sooner or later you will crack this.

So, having talked about the situational relationship with alcohol, which <u>creates</u> the climate when drinking becomes a coping mechanism, let's talk about how your situation can get you out of that hole?

If you are reading this book, it is pretty clear that you have either decided or are debating changing your relationship with alcohol. If you have already started on the freedom path, congratulations.

Whether you have started or are yet to start, this book is about acknowledging that you drink, or drank, for a reason and that reason was positive. Read that again. The reason behind your drinking was positive. Don't tell yourself that you are or were a terrible person. Misguided, yes. Terrible – no.

Don't beat yourself up. You drink/drank to cope. However, there are better ways to cope and this book is about more positive habits and practices so when you kick the crutch of alcohol away, you are not left wobbling on one leg.

What is your pay off for not drinking or cutting down?

The "Why?" is really, really important. Here I am re-printing my list of pay offs for being AF:

- ability to function at all times of day

- freedom from obsessing about what, when and where to drink

- energy freed from obsessing

- better health

- more interesting life

- better relationships with my family

- honest emotions – honestly happy and unhappy and everything in between

- more free time to do interesting and enjoyable things

Think about your own list. Give yourself permission to think about what it will be like to be free.

My list is a combination of "towards" and "away" things:

Towards goals are things that inspire you and that you want. For example, different hobbies or better health. Away goals are things, the elements of drinking that have just become unmanageable. For example the hangovers or rows with loved ones or low mood or the self-criticism on a loop that you hear in your head each morning after the night before.

You don't need both types of goals or even a long list. The list just needs to be personal, how you really feel.

I talk about goal setting in Chapter Four. Making goals stick is very much about being clear about your own "whys", your own list of what you want to get away from or move towards as an AF person.

If there is any upside in the bleak moods that alcohol brings on (be under no misunderstanding, alcohol is causing you to feel low, it is not the other way round), it is the best opportunity to write down how alcohol or hangovers make you feel or be and the effect that it is having on your life. These are some of your "away from" goals, so add them to your list.

In more cheerful moments, or when a drink sounds or looks or feels like a good idea, all those negatives that you feel in your soul the morning after the night before or even as the drinking night wore on, dissolve like gossamer threads to your resolve. You forget the bad stuff. So, write down your whys as part of the goals setting in Chapter Four so you are very clear why you want to change your relationship with alcohol. Keep that list and get it out if you start to gloss over the bad times. You can even do yourself a personal video blog and keep that for your danger times. You can put it on YouTube and keep it private if you don't want to keep it on your phone. You don't need to show your list to anyone. This is between drinking you and sober you. Let the conversation commence.

This book is not full of plans and checklists. I have a virtual chemical reaction to checklists, they just turn me off. But one thing I did in the first year was keep a notebook with me, which I could pull out to write thoughts. So there was no requirement to write every day and at my most prolific, I wrote maybe three times a week. The notebook sat in my handbag so I could pull it out on the train or while having a sandwich. There was no set time when I would write things in it. But I did find it helpful to note things I learnt about myself as I went along.

I also wrote a blog (which I am going to publish, hopefully this year) and I used my journal to note ideas for themes or quotes or things I saw or heard which amused me or inspired me.

Feel free to use a notebook or even a more formal journal or a blog.

The structure of this book

Chapter 1 has five steps to set the scene:

1. Step 1 Take care of yourself

2. Step 2 Find things to do that do not involve alcohol

3. Step 3 Get yourself organised

4. Step 4 Eat to relieve stress

5. Step 5 Focus on long term changes one step at a time.

These are mindset commitments which help you succeed.

Some of them may be a surprise.

For example: the idea in Step 2 that you need to get out and connect with people rather than hide under a duvet while not drinking, may not be your first choice. But the opposite of addiction or reliance is not abstinence, it is **connection**. A self-defeating habit, like reliance on alcohol, closes your world down. You need to open it up again and take the focus off alcohol.

Chapters Two and Five discuss the part that what you eat can play in getting and staying alcohol free. Chapter Five suggests what to eat having had Chapter Two set up the framework of what a better diet might look like for you.

As I said earlier, the *"Just eat healthily"* advice is fine but we need a bit more than that to take account of our urge towards alcohol and our need to replace a negative coping mechanism with a better one. How many times have you read the advice "If you think you are drinking too much, just alternate alcoholic drinks with non-alcoholic ones or have two to three alcohol free days a week?" Well, that advice is useless. If we could have done that, we would have done that.

I have completely re-written these chapters to take account of the research on sugar and relapse and sugar and mood. Most of the research in this field is based on work with prison inmates and youths in detention, which gives it a certain curiosity as a law abiding member of society but we have to thank them for their situation because they are a captive survey group. They are also a fertile group for alcohol dependence and negative behaviours. The research on diet's link with heavy drinking, relapse, depression and aggression is both fascinating and massively encouraging for what you can do with diet to almost guarantee your success Chapter Five is the plan for what to eat to feel better. The advice tells you how to structure your nutrition, what healthy looks like if you have been a drinker, and how to get back to better health and what particular foods to eat.

I have also expanded the comment on Supplements in Chapter Six in conversation with a nutritionist, Maia Lloyd. My publisher, Three Peas (www.threepeaspublishing.com) has a nutritionist, Maia Lloyd writing for them and she provided very helpful feedback and resources to expand the comment on Chapters Five, Six and Seven

I hope you enjoy these chapters and feel buoyed by them.

Chapter Three is about your inner, mental life and introduces the idea of a Morning Ritual to help set your positive mindset. You may not have come across this before: the idea that a positively chosen ritual first thing will help you. You may think it is too hard or that you have no time. As I discuss in the chapter, if you don't plan your ritual, you have one anyway but it is likely to be reactive and not supportive of the levels of fulfilment and happiness you want now. So have a read and see what you can do for you.

Chapter Four is my Ten Laws of Sober resilience. This is the toolbox of behaviours based on advice from coaching to neuro linguistic programming to mindfulness.

Ten ways to support your decision to dial down alcohol and feel better.

You can use all of them and I challenge you to try all of them and see what works for you.

My Ten Laws of Sober Resilience give you ten alternatives to alcohol.

Ten other ways to cope.

You may already be doing some of these or none. I challenge you to say that all ten, you have done or all ten you have tried and they do not help.

The aim of the chapter is to help you find skills that work for you.

It is the main coaching chapter with ideas to help your mindset.

Chapter Six is about supplements for body repair, mood and cravings. This is prefaced by the warning that you should see your doctor or get a nutritionist for more detailed prescribing although there is also advice on basic use of supplements to support recovery.

Chapter 7 Explains particular foods to target supporting your liver and "Love Your Liver" Recipes. These recipes are indicative as the approach I have taken is to give you the information on what foods you need in your diet but left it up to you to decide how you do that.

There is then a section on my other books in this series which help you get and stay AF and details of some free downloads of books.

The one book that I would highlight here is my Amazon Best Seller called "Alcohol Top Ten Cravings Busters". It is five star rated and has had some great reviews. I think it has done well because it gathers the advice on how to avoid cravings and switch them off, all in one place and sticks to that focus – solutions not war stories. So it is similar to this book in terms of trying to ease the path to being AF by getting all the helpful information in one place.

You can find this book on Amazon if you search "Top Ten Cravings Busters by Catherine Mason Thomas" and if you are reading this book on a tablet or PC, here is the Amazon link

http://www.amazon.com/dp/B01C4G85MW

Here are the most recent, Amazon all five star, customer reviews

Customer Reviews of Cravings Busters

By marion on 10 April 2016
Format: Kindle Edition Verified Purchase
Some very useful tips for managing cravings especially in the early days of sobriety. She does include people who want to moderate their drinking as well as those who want to give up altogether.

By A Customer on 12 April 2016
Format: Kindle Edition Verified Purchase
Really found this easy to read and didn't make me feel as though I was a lost cause!! A lot of other 'Alcohol' related books have made me feel like a loser and that there is no way out. The advice is to the point with some really helpful advice and tips

By The_Urban_Muse on 11 May 2016
Format: Kindle Edition Verified Purchase
This is short, punchy and humorous. I tend to get bored with the repetitive books; they seem to infer that they act as some sort of subliminal message (almost hypnotic), but I can't get into them, as I keep thinking that I've already read that bit!
Neither does the author dwell anyone's morose past, with alcohol induced tales of woe (I do enjoy reading these books too, as I'm a nosy old bat!). Ultimately it is down to the individual, as no one can wave a magic wand, and you will be, "Cured!" It does offer some good coping strategies for beating the cravings.

By m on 18 April 2016
Format: Kindle Edition Verified Purchase
Very helpful and motivational

The last part of this book is My Conclusion: my closing thoughts. It's a rara to get you going or keep you on track. I wish I could be

there with you to cheer you on but this book is the next best thing.

You are making the best decision of your life, don't doubt that. Let's just talk about what had held you back.

What is holding you back?

There are lots of reasons for transferring your allegiance from alcohol to other self-supporting habits.

What holds us back is fear that nothing will do it for us like alcohol has. What you may not have accepted fully with your head and your heart is that there are positive ways to get the same support you get from alcohol. You do not have to pour alcohol down your throat to get the same emotional relief.

This book will give you lots of self-supporting habits to replace alcohol with. Things that support how you feel emotionally and physically.

If you take alcohol out, it will be worth it very quickly. Within days of stopping drinking, you will feel better. Just build on that day by day. It is a bit like those children's clay eggs you get with a little hammer and you are meant to chip away at the clay to reveal the plastic dinosaur. If you did it all in one go, you would drive yourself mad hammering away. A better strategy is to do a bit a day, just so long as you do not put it aside and forget about it.

One strategy is to diarize each day, fifteen minutes or half an hour for things associated with your commitment to being AF or cutting down. I used to write a blog most mornings. That was my time to reflect and write down how things were going. I used to write my feelings down so if I was not having a very hot day, getting it on paper or a computer screen helped. Use the time you set aside, that fifteen or thirty minutes, to pick a strategy, emotional or nutritional and have a go at using the tools in this book to change things or help yourself along.

That may sound like a time commitment which you do not have. But remember all that drinking time. I know what time pressure is like, I used to multi-task drinking and housework. I am not sure if I thought I was being efficient or if doing the washing and cleaning the loo at the same time distracted me.

Once you take out the self-limiting habit that alcohol is, you create the space in your life for other things. You will seek out beauty, in the form of new or deeper relationships, better food, new interests and/or a greater acceptance of yourself and your emotional range. This is a spreading of wings and flight, just like a butterfly emerging from its chrysalis. In the initial stages, a chunk of that free time will be for getting yourself in shape, mentally and emotionally so use a note book or a blog, choose a tool from this book, maybe a morning ritual and just see what works for you.

There will be self-doubt and temptations along the way as you break the alcohol habit. Nothing scary. This book will make the journey easier and more enjoyable.

Getting the life you want

As I said in Edition 1 – I think the difference between stopping drinking and committing to being sober long term is the difference between staying away from the next drink and embracing a new life made possible because you don't drink.

Your life should not be "minus" alcohol. Your life should be "plus" things you could not or did not have the confidence or drive to do when alcohol took up a prominent part of your life.

This book is about getting the life you want, part of which is and is fueled by the way you approach your inner life and the way you approach nutrition. You can't look and feel your best if you are in inner turmoil or you are eating food that is bad for you.

This book is about us out the other side of drinking and looking to the future. This book is about how what we choose to think and feel and eat helps us live the life of our dreams - enough energy, positivity and attitude to take on anything.

If you have stopped drinking, you will have proved to yourself that you can do anything if you focus on it.

Now that you are through the initial, all out concentration of just not taking that first drink, it is time to open out your life and decide what else you want to go for or change.

If you are reading this, it is a safe bet that you want to up your emotional and nutritional game. I am with you. Your attitude and nutrition and looking after yourself is part of the growing up you do when the party stops.

This book will give you sound advice on what you can do with your mental approach and nutrition to support your recovery.

What sort of advice is in this book?

There are lots of guides to happiness, mindfulness and healthy eating out there and they are all helpful and helped me to sort out what would assist me to feel and look better.

My own skills in my field I have brought to this book in considering how to help with the mental element of change.

My research which took on an inevitable focus on habits to replace alcohol still surprised me. I learnt about mindfulness and shifting your emotional state at will, to create some of the positive pay offs from drinking.

Mental shifts I had thought reserved for taking something, such as alcohol, could be created with nutrition and positive emotional practices.

When I starting reading into goal setting in sobriety, I could not find anything that gave me a menu of practices in emotional health, mindfulness or mastery and nutrition following an alcohol habit. I do like a manual.

They say now that people have almost everything they want, except time. I wanted to have tools for AFness (is that a word?) in one place. The answers were scattered across books on emotional health, mindfulness, nutrition, NLP. Few of these books addressed becoming AF and I thought that was an important slant on these approaches. A lot of the standard advice applies but there are tweaks you need to make to take into account alcohol history.

For the emotional side, you are coming out of a bleak or certainly negative place. You may not even realise how much of a depressant alcohol is until you take it out. Or, you may be all too aware of the damage that alcohol has done to your emotional health and self-esteem: you may have done things that are way below the standards you expect of yourself. You need to be kind to yourself and accept that you are not perfect and perfectionism is not your driver.

There is a lot of fear around cravings and relapse and the combined weight of media coverage of the alcoholic failures in our society serves to make the future look extremely unstable in terms of staying sober. How much easier to just stay where you are: unpleasant, depressive but familiar?

But if you take encouragement from what I have said in this Introduction about the situational factors that lead to heavy drinking and the situational factors you can employ to support your pull back from this, this book will give you lots of support to get you started or getting running along the alcohol free path.

The other part of this book is about Nutrition. In terms of nutrition, healthy eating advice is good advice for everyone, including the former heavy drinker. As a qualified personal trainer, nutritional guidance is part of my skill set. I did however have to do quite a lot of research when it came to putting together a program for myself as I passed along recovery.

Someone who has not used alcohol as a coping mechanism cannot really understand the mindset that needs more than the advice "Eat healthily". We all know that.

I was looking for advice on what could ease the path, support my emotional resolve and positive feelings and help me manage any cravings.

So, this book goes beyond the standard advice and talks about:

1. Foods that assist your body's recovery from alcohol;

2. Eating habits that help avoid and manage the risk of relapse and the onset of a craving

3. Supplements that help healing from alcohol damage

4. Supplements that support positive emotions

5. Some specific recipes that include the foods you should be eating

I hope that this book will encourage you to take charge of your mental attitude and diet or take it up a notch so you are doing specific things to help your mind and body recover from the assault of alcohol.

The good news is that virtually all the damage done by alcohol can be reversed with time and good nutrition.

You can wake up happy to be alive and raring to go. You can sustain that positive attitude and energy levels all day and then sleep well at night.

I invite you to go for the best rest of your life possible and that is far more happy and successful than you need to settle for right now.

The third goal of this book, beyond supporting you in being alcohol free and giving you the tools in terms of positive practice and nutritional support to get and stay alcohol free, is to help you decide and go for what you really want your life to be when you are free of alcohol dependence.

Read this book and implement some of the advice. Look back in a year's time at how much you have changed your life for the better. I hope your life in a year's time is unrecognizable to what it is now. You deserve it.

Here is to the rest of our lives, alcohol free and experience rich.

You can also find lots of health advice, recipes and videos via my publisher's website www.threepeaspublishing.com and YouTube channel "Three Peas Media".

Now let's get on to Chapter 1

Catherine Mason Thomas

Chapter 1

Five steps to alcohol freedom

If you have got yourself in a mess with alcohol, you are most likely not shouting about that.

You are more likely keeping it to yourself.

Any sort of addiction, obsession or dependency is isolating.

Recovery means building meaningful and productive connections with people, proper connections with friends, workmates and family members. It comes back to: What is the opposite of alcohol dependency? It is not freedom, it is connection.

I should have called this chapter "Connection" but most people think about getting free of the weight of a dependency. It is only later, as our worlds open out again and we start to live a richer, more varied and, let's face it, less boring, existence that the penny drops that drinking is a lonely life, even when surrounded by people.

The two connections you will cultivate will be external and internal: Having meaningful connections through relationships and looking after yourself are the two forms of connection. I had the urge to get a pet so followed the AA rule – no new relationships for two years. I know they meant romantic relationships but I concluded that having the commitment of a dog was also a bad idea this early into sober life.

Having a positive internal relationship with yourself. Feeling good about yourself and rebuilding your self-esteem is important to embed your new habits. What you have achieved and you should be applauding yourself for stopping drinking or pulling it back, is precious and in the early stages, precarious.

You need a plan for supporting your new sober lifestyle. This is your clear idea of what you need to do or practice to embed your new AF lifestyle.

This plan has five steps:

Step 1: Take proper care of yourself. This means managing and eradicating mood swings and meeting and surmounting alcohol and sugar cravings. Ensuring that you have slept properly and eaten foods that are restorative and healthy gives you the resilience you need. This book will give you all the knowledge you need to get this step right.

The other thing that you need to incorporate is proper exercise: this will help in relieving stress, detoxing by stimulating your lymph system, releasing endorphins as well as promoting emotional well-being.

Step 2: Find things to do that do not involve alcohol. You can nurse an orange juice at the pub quiz or a non-alcoholic cocktail at the local bar but it is not much fun in the early days. It is also a real strain on your self-control while you build your AF or moderate life. It can feel a bit like going to your own wake.

You will have moments of grief for the good bits of your old drinking life. Chances are, these moments are cleaned up versions of what really went on since you are stopping or cutting down for a reason. Were the times really that good? Maybe the first drink but what about later on?

If you are in places that you associate with good times, even if your mind has to do mental yoga to ignore all the downsides of your drinking, why put yourself through that strain?

The AA advice and I think it is really sensible, is to avoid people, places and things which you associate with alcohol. You can even chuck out or swap clothing which was your pub gear, wine glasses or cocktail paraphernalia and anything else that talks to you from that life.

I went as far as changing my hair colour. My reason? I associated the colour with my old, brittle, having it all while powering on alcohol self. A year after I became AF, I walked into a hair salon with three of my children and asked them to dye it back to what I suspected was its natural colour. I found it an immense relief to say goodbye to the woman who had been smiling on the outside whilst dying on the inside. I wanted my natural colour back (I had not seen that since I was fifteen) to signify in very outwardly obvious terms, that I wanted nothing hidden, nothing manufactured anymore.

You don't have to go as far as me of course, although some outward demonstration of change is a good thing. The real point is to find activities that you enjoy that are fresh, with no connection to your old habits.

The areas people fish in are often sport, theatre and cinema, cooking, but whatever you can think of.

I remember seeing an interview with comedian Frank Skinner perhaps a year after he had stopped drinking. Now he is a funny man and has made his career being the bitter, twisted one, rather like Tony Hancock. Frank Skinner was asked what hobbies he had and he answered that he had tried virtually everything since he stopped drinking. He delivered the line with a pained expression on his face, as if he was only doing other things because he could not go down the pub. I really hope that was for comedic effect because if you see AF activities as a poor substitute for the bad old days, there is trouble ahead for your AF life.

I can say with hand on breast Brownie style that I have never gone out and done something wanting all the time to be at the pub. I went to a pub a couple of times after I became AF and I found it gruesome. I was not sad that my life had changed, I was relieved. I could not wait to leave on those evenings.

The things I did instead, I went out and did things that I had always wanted to do: riding horses, going to comedy clubs, spending time with my children unhung over. I met people who had never known me as a drinker and the sorts of things I was doing, the subject never came up because alcohol was not in the plan.

I also got involved in an AF social network. I will talk about this more under my Ten Laws in Chapter Five. AF social networks have the advantage that you can be completely honest about the changes you are making and the friends you make will understand.

So, use AF activities to help you build connections and a support network.

Avoid holing yourself up as if on hunger strike while you tough out abstinence. You need more connection not less. Your surroundings will change as you are not going to be focusing on drinking, you are over that.

Surround yourself with people of purpose. They don't have to be alcohol free, although the setting should be. Ensure that you have social connection with and with whom you can socialize without having to drink.

If you are thinking to yourself, but all my friends drink. Hmm.. This can be a challenge, if your social life is built around drinking. That is going to have to change. Drinking buddies are not going to help.

Or, you may be absolutely bored with your life and want a change anyway. Your drinking buddies, or some of them, may be ready for a change too.

Your friends don't have to be on the AF or moderate path but if they are prepared to leave the pub to see you, great! Otherwise, you need to move on.

You may have to be the catalyst for change and see what your friends do.

So check out other things that interest you and invite your friends to those. This will keep you on the recovery track as well as ensure that you are motivated. Meals in and out shared with friends is going to be a big part of that. I took to stand-up comedy (in the audience, not on stage) as something that made me feel good and definitely better tasted sober.

You have no idea how many of the audience, and the comics, are drunk but that is a shame as the comedy, if it's clever, needs to be got sober. I think if you are a comedian, being AF must be like being the only Muslim at a hog roast. What are you going to do?

So, we should think ourselves lucky that our lives have AF chinks in them that we can exploit. Then again, Frank Skinner was even more successful once he stopped drinking and he became more prolific. Dean Martin was also a light drinker despite the image. His drinks on stage were non-alcoholic and when he was drinking with the rat pack, he used to chuck his in the house plants when no-one was looking.

Come to think if it, a huge number of comedians had or have dependency problems. Robin Williams was another.

But I digress...

Choose alcohol free activities to open out our life. Worst case, try and keep trying different things until you find things that you love.

One comment here: you will probably get opposition or even friends who try to persuade you to come to the pub or bar.

There is absolutely nothing which says that you have to declare yourself an alcoholic to everyone as an opener to asking them to meet at a restaurant rather than the said pub or bar.

As I said in the Introduction, you don't have to declare yourself anything, it is your business. It depends on your make up and your relationships.

Some people need to confide and are confident that they have supportive people who, armed with the knowledge, will help, not hinder.

Others know or suspect that family or friends will oppose and use guerrilla tactics to stop change, to the extreme of spiking drinks or bringing alcohol round.

So you judge it but don't feel obligated to share. There is no qualification for stopping drinking or entry level you have to qualify for. You don't need to wear a badge or have some liver shaped smart card which entitles you to avoid all drinking places. It is your business and no-one else's.

If you are worried about what other people think, remember the saying *"What other people think about you in none of your business"*.

Worst case, just smile and then ignore them.

If you need a non-confrontational, public reason, play the health card. Say you are on a diet or a new healthy eating plan and alcohol is out. Sooner or later your friends will see that you are not drinking period, and if they ask you can decide what you tell them, eventually they won't even question it so it becomes a non-subject.

Step 3: **Get yourself organized.** One of the problems with drinking is that it wipes out time and motivation to take care of some of the basics in your life. Letters are not answered, internet banking not organized, family responsibilities not assumed.

I remember going to see a club for troubled teenagers as a potential donor. We were shown round and one of the most impressive things was the remains of a training session they had run that morning. There was a large sheet of white paper ripped off an even larger roll. It has been laid on the ground and the outline of a person drawn, crime scene style. The figure had then been hung vertically as a representative person and the teenagers asked to write on the figure what it meant to be a good citizen. Apart from the obvious, like not shooting up the neighbourhood or holding up old ladies, someone had written the phrase "pay your taxes". I was really struck by the rightness of that.

I am not here to ask you what your motivations are for dialing down alcohol but one of mine was definitely growing up and taking care of personal business.

One of the first things I did with my sober evenings was to devise a proper filing system for all my home paperwork. I know, I know. It's not Rock 'n Roll. But you know what? It still gives me an immense sense of calm when I look at my files and know that I am now one of the more organized people I know. It also makes me shudder, how long I could have continued with the chaos bubbling.

So, work out what growing up means to you. Look at what you have shortcutted in favour of a drink and put things right. It will give you more self-esteem than a dozen drinks, I promise you.

Also a word here about volunteering: Get to work in areas that have got purpose and meaning to your life and engage in volunteer activities. Focusing on others is a great way to add meaning to your life and in terms of fulfilment, it is the only real route of true happiness. This is not me being trite, it is a fact.

Even if you do not agree that helping others will give you a better feeling than alcohol, the act of engaging in any new activities means no time for drinking in your life so have a go..

Step 4 – Eat to relieve stress. I do not mean stress eat! I mean choose foods that help to keep you calm and resilient and avoid cravings.

Chapters 2 and 5 go into detail about how and what to eat to stabilize your moods, rebuild your health and look so much better.

I meet people now who, despite me maybe not having brushed my hair for several days (four kids, no time – my excuse), no make-up and little sleep due to toddlers, they tell me how well I look. I still forget that what they are talking about is the lack of redness and puffiness that you develop if you drink. If you don't drink, you automatically look better, your skin is clear and you look leaner and brighter.

We will get to what to eat and supplement to really get you on form but in the meantime, in this step, the priority is to keep your moods stable so you feel positive and committed to the change you are making.

The secret is to manage your blood sugar. In case you didn't know, alcohol is a sugar (I am not meaning to patronize, see below what I had kidded myself about alcohol).

You have been tipping sugar into your system via your drinking. Now you have stopped or created a serious sugar shortage.

I really had myself convinced that ethanol metabolized differently from sugar so I was not doing anything to my blood sugar. It is amazing what a little nutritional knowledge combined with denial can come up with. I thought that because I was slim, the alcohol could not possibly be sugar. Of course, I was ignoring one of the side effects of alcohol, it suppresses your appetite.

I also preferred to drink on an empty stomach to get a bigger "hit". Many drinkers save their calories to "spend" on alcohol. I know now that this behaviour, also known as alcorexia is particularly damaging to your organs as they are working hard for you dealing with a poison with minimal nutritional help.

When we stop drinking or cut right down, the body goes *"Where did the sugar go?"*

Most diet advice has no idea the shock you put your body through when you exclude or minimize alcohol after a committed drinking habit. The usual advice "Eat more fruit and vegetables" does not really cut it.

The priority is to keep your energy and mood stable and to do this you need to watch your sugar, period. It does not matter if it is the sugar from a chocolate bar or a slice of pineapple, it is still sugar. I do think that some versions of healthy eating out there are incredibly high in sugar. Tipping a shed load of sugar, whether it's called fruit, honey, brown rice syrup or coconut nectar, into your diet is not a good idea, partiularly when the body is craving it..
The things to watch out for in your new, healthy diet are:

Fructose – from fruit;
Maple syrup – has healthy minerals but is still sugar;
Brown rice syrup – think of it as syrup dressed up as healthy. Eveything is relative I suppose and compared to golden syrup it is;
Coconut sugar/nectar – it may be called "nectar" but it still counts as sugar;

Grape juice/apple juice – a common sweetener added to health store snacks;

Dates – most 'healthy' cookies and brownies are sweetened with these. Yes, they have useful minerals, but they are very high in sugar;

Agave syrup – this is a tricky one. It's a syrup processed from cacti. The jury is still out on how this affects your body. It may process in your body like sugar. I find that it affects my mood just like sugar. So take care with agave. See how you feel emotionally a few hours after eating it. Even if you feel fine, do not go overboard with agave; and

Stevia and xylitol – Less of a concern as they are both derived from natural sources and have both been shown not to affect blood sugar, but that doesn't mean you can use a ladle with them. Xylitol, if eaten to excess, can also cause stomach discomfort.

I use some fruit, Stevia and agave, but in moderation.

So, although you need to be eating natural foods and fruit in particular is a good part of that, it is important to balance the natural sugars in your diet by including proteins and fats too. Proteins help stabilise your blood sugar, preventing the roller-coaster ride that can cause cravings and low mood Fats stop your stomach emptying so you feel full.

The easiest way to stay balanced is to make sure every meal and snack includes carbs, proteins and fats together. If you want to do a juice, add some yoghurt for protein and some Chia seeds for health fats or add some Omega 3 oil. If you're making a salad, boil an egg to go with it and chuck in some walnuts to get your protein. You get the idea.

Step 5 – Focus on long term changes but one step at a time. You don't need to do everything at once. Just start.

It may help you if you think of your commitment to being alcohol free as being for a set period. Think Dry January or Sober September.

That is different from saying to yourself "*I will give this a try*".

You are not trying and to use an AA phrase *"Trying is lying"*.

So you need to commit to the changes being permanent but you can salami slice the time if permanent sounds too scary.

I don't know anyone who regrets taking a break from alcohol. I know plenty who regret either drinking or what they have done drunk.

A good book to read is "The One" by Seth Godin. This is a management book but it applies to anything you are trying to achieve. The book has great comment on self-control and the absolute need to focus on one thing. If the one thing for you is changing your life by changing your relationship with alcohol – that is what you concentrate on.

I genuinely believe that drinking is a bad habit rather than some insurmountable, demonic possession. Drinking is compulsive so you need to interrupt the loop with new things and new habits.

A new habit takes on average sixty two days to implant although The One quotes research that says the more difficult the target, the longer it takes to embed the change.

But it does not stay as hard.

It is not white knuckle, blood on the walls climb to Mount Everest stuff every day. It gets easier quickly, within two weeks, I think. By a year, you should be in the groove and be doing other, more interesting stuff and feeling relieved that your new habit seems to be settling down.

So that is the Five Step framework to how I suggest to approach altering your relationship with alcohol.

This book will give you far more to aim for in terms of your potential and happiness from Chapter Four onwards.

I just want to say that by already making it to this page, it shows that you have a passion and an urge, deep down inside of you, to make your sobriety the start of even more positive change in your life! I congratulate you for on aspiring to more. So once again, congratulations to you for stopping drinking or cutting back. Give yourself a pat on the back, you deserve it!

Now onto Chapter Two and how what you eat can help you stay sober.

Chapter 2

Staying sober – the part that nutrition can play

This chapter sets out the principles for a diet to help you get and stay AF or moderate. Chapters Five and Six get into the detail.

You may have drunk for all sorts of reasons often several at once (reasons, not drinks) – to relax, to give you confidence, to make you feel better, to pep you up, to put you to sleep, and many others. Whatever your perceived pay off from having a drink, you got to the stage when that pay off either was not there or the downsides of drinking just made it not workable anymore.

You decided to stop drinking, possibly for the umpteenth time, this time it stuck and you are now proudly a non-drinker. You have gone through a similar process to regain balance with alcohol so you are now a moderate drinker.

In either case, well done to you. If you are not there yet, trust that you will be and get started.

You have committed to staying sober or moderating, either forever or one day at a time, or anything between that. You are settled on that path.

How what you eat helps

One of the habits that overhangs from your drinking days – poor nutrition.

There are of course health freaks who drink. There is a tendency to think of health as a set of scales, so if you eats lots of vegetables, that makes up for the excess alcohol. I am afraid that that is not true. If you drink hazardously, as you know, your risk of all sorts of cancers increases, not to mention dementia and cirrhosis. For example, 30% of throat cancer patients are hazardous drinkers.

Having a portion of spinach is not going to change that.

Your health outcomes are not an overall score, like dressage where you get a combined score for pace, form etc.

Drinking increases your risks for some scary diseases, that is it. No argument.

Your motivation for sorting out what you eat may also be linked to wanting more from sobriety. Your move away from alcohol may be part of a general house cleaning you are doing, perhaps linked to a significant event, like a birthday or a divorce (celebration or commiseration?).

Or you have set yourself some physical targets for your new life – to lose a few pounds, run a race or just feel better in your head and skin.

You have come to this book hoping that what you eat can help you achieve your goals.

Nutrition absolutely can help you, if you know what to eat.

Base Camp – What has alcohol left behind?

Let's start with what alcohol, as a form of nutrition, did to you first.

Alcohol is a depressant, although at first it can temporarily lift your mood.

A theory of why alcohol is a downer is that imbibing diminishes how much tryptophan, an amino acid, reaches the brain. Tryptophan is the precursor of serotonin, the happy hormone that the brain produces, which promotes a sense of well-being. Eating carbohydrates, such as grains or chocolate, makes more tryptophan available, which is why women often crave carbohydrate just before a period when they can feel low. It is also why, when you go alcohol free, without the sugar in the form of ethanol (alcohol), we often crave sugar and feel low without it.

So we know that nutrition can help with mood. The previous chapter talked about stabilizing your blood sugar and how this can prevent energy and mood highs and lows. That is key to preventing cravings and supporting your positive mood.

This book is for you as you dial down alcohol or eradicate it from your life so we are concentrating on how we can support mood to support long term recovery. There are some specifics about alcohol addiction and its symptoms which mean that nutrition should be tailored for alcohol recovery.

If a high sugar and junk diet, whatever it did to the general population, actually cured alcohol cravings or made us happy all the time, I would be suggesting that you load up on chocolate and cakes. But, sorry, sugar is not your friend in sobriety, it is your enemy.

At the most basic level, alcohol recovery is supported by having regular meals to help control unstable blood sugar levels, an issue for the great majority of drinkers and a condition that can continue even after drinking has ceased.

Certain foods improve digestion and enhance the absorption of nutrients and we deal with these as we go through the recipes.

That is important because the bodily processes employed to manage alcohol in the body uses up nutrients, so we are likely to be deficient before we start.

In addition, for some people, avoiding foods they are sensitive to can lower the risk of relapse, if they are in a habit of turning to alcohol to ease the symptoms of food allergy, like IBS. This may sound ridiculous but I certainly found that if I felt bloated, the first glass of wine would flatten my tummy. Also, eating foods to which you are either allergic or intolerant, releases psychotropic chemicals into your system and this gives you a sort of "high". In that state, you are more likely to reach for the other high with which you are familiar, alcohol.

The good news is that what you choose to eat can help you stay away from alcohol. Eating better will improve your health to such an extent that life itself becomes more manageable, removing stress that can increase the chance that you may reach for a drink. Good nutrition can increase your energy and mental clarity and help steady your mood, making it easier to get through the day.

The worse your former diet, the greater the chance you'll soon be feeling better as you switch to recovery foods.

General glucose intolerance can persist for a period of time during abstinence until your body recovers, which unfortunately can put you at risk for relapse: low blood sugar creates a craving for anything that will rapidly raise the level of blood sugar, such as cookies, candy, a sugary cola—or an alcoholic drink.

Try to avoid these cravings by choosing protein and fats to help you keep your glucose levels stable.

Of course, everyone's path of recovery is unique, with your own challenges and roadblocks. Give food a chance to help you heal. You might be surprised by the support it can give you.

Chapter 3

Building your sober persona from the inside out

If you do want to get free of alcohol, you do have to commit and then act. All the wishing and resolving in the world is not going to get you over the sober line without action. Knowledge is not power, action is power (you can see my coaching background kicking in).

I think the simplest way to look at it is to believe absolutely that you will not drink and that nothing, no provocation, no mood, no pressure, no temptation, will get you to drink.

You cannot be half-hearted but it is not all hard work. All the way along your alcohol-free path, you will have times of pure elation at the relief and joy of not drinking. I am not exaggerating this. The utter relaxation of not filling your head with the "should I/shouldn't I" debate: the endless planning and preparing to drink and the recovery from drinking. That is all gone.

Building the sober person you want to be requires energy and focus. But you have proved that you are easily up to the task and the goal: you - is worth it.

I will give my comments on what the professionals say about the psychology of precisely how change happens but first, I would like to introduce you to the idea that the first part of the day is the crucial time for embedding or confirming the promises you have made to yourself and the change that you want to happen.

I have to say that not drinking, you are like a missile aimed at your target- the best life you can imagine. The foundation for that and the way that you ground that every day is in – a Morning Ritual.

This can be 2 minutes, 5, 10 or 15, whatever time you can spare.

I have four children plus working so I do know that mornings are busy. But, I always do a version of the ritual at the start of my day. The rewards are so huge that I am committed to it.

I will explain:

A morning ritual is a period first thing in the morning when you mentally center yourself for the day and put yourself in a good mood.

You may think you don't have time for a ritual or that this is a load of new age mumbo jumbo. Well, if you don't take control of this part of the day, you still have a morning ritual but it probably goes like this

Wake up to alarm. Not ready to face the day so hit the snooze (possibly multiple times) Get up at the last minute in a bit of a daze. Listen to the news – wars and death. Think about everything you have to do and have a rushed shower. Coffee to cause a sugar and adrenaline rush. Breakfast, organise kids if you have them, leave and start your working day.

That does not sound like a great way to start the rest of your life, which is what the morning is.

This is what my ideal Morning Ritual looks like

My Morning Ritual
1. Smile on waking
2. Breathing exercises – either nasal or stomach. 3 sets of 20.

3. Breathing and gratitude
4. 2 glasses of water
5. Exercise/comedy/reading
6. Body brush then Shower with 30 second cold cycle
7. Review diary and write down major tasks to be completed today
8. Review and affirm personal goals and my mission statement
9. Travelling or in office while modelling desired emotional states:
   A. energy and positivity
   B. bravery
   C. creativity
   D. calm and connectedness to family and things
10. Give thanks for and celebrate the day and say a prayer

This looks like a lot and is the ideal if I have about an hour. That is a perfect morning which happens possibly twice a week.

If I have five minutes max, I will do steps 1, 2, 3, 4 (smile, breathe, drink,), have a shower, dress while listening to something inspirational from one of my subscribed for podcasts or a TEDs talk (check both out in the App Store) and then do the gratitude (gives thanks, celebrate and pray) as I walk to my train station.

Of all of the elements, the one that has the greatest effect on my mood is the smile on waking. They have done research on mood and even asking people to hold a pencil between their teeth, which you can only do by lifting the smile muscles around your mouth, improves people's moods. That is definitely my experience. So, whatever time you have, try a real or forced smile first thing and see what it does to your mood and wait to be amazed.

Maybe start with the smile and then start to build some other elements in. I cannot stress how big a difference this ritual has made to my mood, confidence and centeredness. Even on the worst days, I might feel a bit flat but I don't have feelings of downness that persist beyond the ritual. I leave my ritual feeling better than when I started, without fail.

If you want to learn more about creating your own morning ritual, I recommend the online course on morning rituals run by Stefan Pylarnos at www.projectlifemastery.com.

The amazing thing is that it never occurred to me when I drank that I could create a mood shift with thoughts. I assumed that it took external stimuli to change my mood. So if I wanted to feel better, I would apply something to myself, mainly alcohol.

It was been a revelation to realise that you can do a series of things internally designed to create a happy mood and it works.

If you think "I could not get up in time to do any of these", the secret is to get up when the alarm rings, no snooze! If you struggle with getting up in the morning that is a change you can and would be best to make because it gives you time to center your day. The most basic thing is to get to bed at night. If you are short of sleep, you need to catch up at the start of your sleep, not the end. So get to bed earlier and see if that makes it easier to find the time for a ritual in the morning.

If you are still finding it tough to get out of bed on an alarm, you are over thinking this. The problem with getting up is that at the time the alarm goes, you have forgotten your good intentions the night before. That morning state does not need debate or discretion. You need to be robotic – alarm goes and you get up, no debate allowed.

My best tip is to put the alarm across the room and have a glass of water next to the alarm which you drink straight away. This is usually enough to wake me up. The water gets my body going and changes my state from sleep to awake.

Chapter 4

My Ten Laws of Sober Resilience

These ten laws are ten things you can do to make your path easier, support your success and get what you ultimately want: a life beyond alcohol dependence and towards your real human potential and dreams.

I encourage you to try them all but you can take them one or a few at a time. I recommended in the Five Steps in Chapter 1 that you have some time each day to think about how you are doing and look at what else you could do. This is your menu so see what looks good to you and try it.

1. **Have a positive Morning Ritual** (see previous chapter).

2. **Use mindfulness to float over negative emotions**. When your thoughts travel to a dark past or an unknown future, re-capture your thoughts and channel your energy to NOW.

   The present moment is when your power is at its greatest. This type of stepping out of your thoughts, registering that you have them but not getting caught up in them is called Mindfulness. It has been proved to be far more effective with stress management and depression than drugs. It is also extremely effective with cravings.

If you have a negative thought or a feeling of unease, rather than wrestling with it or answering back, register that you have this feeling and be curious to investigate how actually it feels. Float above it like a curious observer or scientist.

This is how you would work mindfulness for alcohol cravings:

Ooh, I have a craving (feeling of unease or ants in your pants which you would in the past have settled with a drink)

How does this particular craving feel in my body and my mind?

Is it a physical sensation or emotional or both?

What is my inner voice saying to me? What is the tone of voice, who does it sound like?

Does this feel like other cravings? Are there elements that are different/the same?

How is my breathing? Fast/slow, shallow/deep?

If you go through this process, it brings you away from the craving to help you calm yourself. It's not distraction as such, it is treating your own self with care and asking your own self what is wrong.

Research on mindfulness used to treat addictive cravings has shown that those who practice mindfulness have fewer cravings and higher levels of overall happiness.

Have a try - There is plenty of mindfulness and meditation

guidance online so have a look and try it. What have you got to lose? There are also some great Apps which take you through mindfulness and meditation programmes. Two I like are called "Calm" and "Be Humble". Be Humble is also about random acts of kindness.

3. **Don't confuse fear with inability**. When we feel fear, we instinctively try to get away from the fear-making situation. That has sound evolutionary reasons but in modern life, most fearful situations are not going to kill us if we stay around.

I used to think that someone who was brave didn't feel fear. I realise now that this was incorrect. The definition of bravery is feeling fear but doing it anyway. Fear can stop you growing and taking risks - don't let it do that. When I was thinking about stopping drinking, what stopped me becoming sober was fear. It was not chemical addiction that stopped me. It was fear. I was afraid of so many things.

That I would not be able to cope without my friend, alcohol

That I would fail

That I would have to come out as an alcoholic and be shamed

That I would dissolve in a puddle of ectoplasm like the ghosts in Ghostbusters due to stress with no alcohol relief

That I would become the person who did not drink because they were weak, weak enough to become an alcoholic

That my reputation would be shot and I would become unemployable

That my children would be embarrassed about me

That is a pretty comprehensive and self-hating list, isn't it?

I overcame these fears and did my Day 1 AF when I read a piece which showed on a graph people's stress levels. The graph showed that people's resting stress levels were far higher if they drank. I did a double take. You feel more stressed <u>because</u> you drink! So my little helper was creating the problem.

Hang on a minute...

I suggest that you write your fears down, just write a list. Just get them out of your head and then tell them that they are there but they will not stop you. Be courageous.

If you are going to write your fears down. The next thing to do it to write the opposing statement. So, for every fear or limiting belief, write down the empowering belief.

To give you an example:

"I will fail" is countered by *"I will succeed"*

I talk more about limiting beliefs and empowering beliefs in Law 7.

Once I have the fears and their counter statements on the page, I decide and write down what I really want to achieve. This is big picture stuff. The direction you want your life to go in. The standard by which you will judge how you are doing and the benchmark against which you will assess decisions to be taken.

So you can get a sense of what a personal mission statement might look like for you, here is mine.

My Mission Statement

To live my fifties in an extraordinary way by doing absolutely everything in my power to live my life in positive states of:

Energy and positivity

Bravery

Creativity

Calm & spirituality

To use those states to create meaning and gratitude through my connection and contribution to my family, friends and strangers

The point about this mission statement is that it gives me a direction for my life.

As a drinker, it is difficult to look beyond the next drinking session. Alcohol has that dumbing down effect. It also raises your anxiety levels so the future, particularly without a drink, seems terrifying.

When I woke up from this, it was because I had a bigger fear. I had this dread of getting to seventy and realising that I had never reached my true potential because I was too busy pouring alcohol down my throat.

Eighteen months sobriety later and I am very clear that I have plans for my future and my mission statement says what I want to be. Because I focus on this statement in my Morning Ritual, I know that it will come true.

Think about what you want to become. An old soak or something more heroic? In mythology there is the concept of a hero's journey. I like this image as getting sober takes mental toughness and willingness to travel into the unknown. Having developed those skills and proved to ourselves that we can triumph over fear, why stop there?

What do you want to be?

Where do you want to go?

How do you want to feel?

4. **Be careful who you share your plans with** There will be skeptics and people opposed to you climbing out of the alcohol pit. People have mixed feelings about your changes because they affect everyone around you. When you change, you change the space between you and other people have to respond to that. Some would prefer things to stay the way they were.

   The skepticism will come out as concern.

   When troubled by skeptics and critics, don't forget the positive people who believed in you. Plus, whatever they say, you remember how bad you felt when you were drinking. Hold onto that.

   Remember the scene in Godfather Part 2 when Marlon Brando says to his son played by Al Pacino, "*When the traitor comes, he will come as your friend. Whoever comes with an offer of peace, he is the traitor you have been looking for."* Or similar words.

I know that is a bit dramatic. I am just counselling you to be wary of gestures of concern or other emotional manipulation from family or friends. Do not be swayed by them. This is your life and your decision.

6. **Get some rest**. When I feel ill at ease or just down in the dumps, I ask my sub-conscious what I need to do to feel better. I literally, lie down on the floor, relax and talk to myself. I ask *"Subconscious, what do I need to do right now to feel better?"*

Often the answer is "sleep"

7. **Use your physiology to change your mood.** Your physiology is how you hold yourself and how you move. Think about how you move when you get great news - you smile, your eyes shine, you lift your chest and may throw your arms out, you may jump or skip on the spot.

Now think about your physiology when you get bad news – you slump, your head is down, eyes downcast, you shallow breath and your limbs are limp.

So physiology is intimately linked to how you feel. To move yourself from one state to another, presumably we would all aim for a happy state, your physiology has to mimic a happy state, and the mood will follow.

Here are examples of desired states and the physiology to help you get there:

Happy- smile, sit up or jump around, pretend that you have just won the lottery – how would you behave?

Confident – smile, steady gaze, shoulders back

Relaxed – steady breathing from your stomach not your chest, open posture with arms at your side

Energetic – animated face, bouncing around

This is part of the reason that my Morning Ritual works to put me in a positive mood. Part of my Ritual mimics the physiology for happiness and energy.

8. **Be positive. Practice "I can means I can. I can't means I can't".** Self-limiting beliefs such as that you can't do something, are tremendously limiting for you and they are so unnecessary. If people can walk across hot coals just with the power of "I can", what can you do that you thought you couldn't? To fight self-limiting beliefs, you begin by acknowledging that you have them. So write them down.

Here is my list of the ones I am aware of at the moment

I have no time to do things I want to do

The children need me to focus on them and I can't do both

It's too late for me to make radical changes

I will look foolish

What if I look stupid?

I have no energy left to take on anything extra

It's all too hard

Having faced your own self-limiting beliefs, you then write down the counter comment – the Empowering Beliefs.

Think about each self-limiting belief and then be your own best friend and answer those with a statement that contradicts it.

Here is an example

Self-limiting belief – *I don't have time to study for [new job/qualification] the children will suffer.*

Empowering belief – *The children will cope. I am building a future for us all and there will never be a perfect time.*

You get the idea.

Here are my empowering beliefs currently written on my wall

My Empowering Beliefs

My goal is to work in a way which liberates time with my family

My family will cope while I build a better life for me

It is my time now

If not now, when?

My perspective is valuable

It does not matter what anyone else thinks

I have proved to myself that I focus on one thing, I can achieve it

Life is growth

I say I can so I can

I am a fast learner

I can break things down to learn them

I can find the need and fill it elegantly

9. **Give yourself a break. No-one is perfect.** They say that addiction is narcissistic because it is an inward focused activity.

   Although to get sober, you have to focus on you, long term sobriety and creating a really positive life requires you to face outwards again and make connections.

   In my mission statement, I refer to connection. I say:

   To use those [emotional states I want to concentrate on] to create meaning and gratitude <u>through my connection and contribution to my family, friends and strangers</u>

   Life without addiction is connection. The opposite of addiction is connection. So you need to get out and interact with people if you want to get away from the thought processes which sucked you down into dependence on alcohol.

   There are also all sorts of social networks now operating to help people get sober and stay sober and to make sober friends.

   Here are some examples to check out:

   Soberistas.com

Hellosundaymorning.com

Sober.meetup.com

Recovery.org

Sobersocial.com

Recoverystreet.com

It is amazing how quickly social networks with a niche of AF living have got going and anyone now deciding to get sober will find it a lot easier if they join one of these sites and take strength and encouragement from other members. There are usually some very experienced, long sober members who will give advice and encouragement for the newbies.

Also, as your own sobriety stretches out, you can help the newbies and in the process be reminded of what you left behind and why you don't drink.

10. **Getting out into nature**. If you are lucky enough to live somewhere that is naturally beautiful, getting out to appreciate it, will rebalance you.

If you live somewhere more brutal than beautiful, take trips into nature regularly. Even a trip to the park will help to rebalance you.

10. **Give back**. Doing something for someone else is the only way to live a joyous life. That is not just me saying it. Research on happiness shows a direct correlation between altruism and personal fulfilment and joy.

You could volunteer or use your work skills to help a charity. If you are on LinkedIn, there is an option in your profile which allows you to highlight your willingness to do work for charity so offers come to you.

You can also do small acts of kindness. Here is my list of random acts of kindness that comes to mind without even trying. You can have your own list but write it down and do them, and see how you feel in a month.

Buy a coffee for a homeless person

Walk an obviously lost person to their destination

Carry an elderly person's shopping/offer to do their shopping or take them to the supermarket

Bake some cookies for your postman and as a minimum, use his name when you meet him on the doorstep

Smile and say hello to a stranger

Give up your seat on the train to someone who looks tired

Pay for someone else's coffee in the coffee bar

Offer to clear up the garden and plant bulbs for an elderly person

Offer to read at a nursing home

So, those are my ten laws. Now on to Chapter Five

Chapter 5

What you eat will make or break your sober goals

So, you know what you want to achieve.

Do you know how nutrition can improve your odds of succeeding?

Let me quote a piece of research:

In 1983 at the University of Texas, researchers asked attendees at Alcoholics Anonymous to split into two groups. Both followed the AA programme but one half also received nutritional advice and education including menu planning, shopping, food prep and how to read food labels.

Six months after discharge from the programme, 81% of the group that got the added nutritional support were not drinking, as compared to 38% who had AA and nothing else. (Gunther 1983)

That is pretty surprising, don't you think?

It should not really be surprising. If you have been drinking to pep yourself up, calm yourself down or anything else, you are already a believer in using what you consume (drink) to change the way you think and feel. The problem with that in alcohol terms is you got more then you bargained for in terms of negative outcomes.

If you adopt the same approach to turning things around, why wouldn't what you eat or drink (nonalcoholic) influence how you think and feel and inevitably what you do as a result?

Let's look at another piece of research: In 1986 another US study looked at inpatient treatment for alcohol dependence. Half the patients got a nutritional program as well. You know where this is going. 33% of the patients in the straight treatment programme were still not drinking six months later. 81% of the patients who had had the nutritional programme as well, were still not drinking (Phelps, Keller & Nourse 1986).

This is really fantastic news. We are pummeled with negative messages about how hard it is to stop drinking. Phrases like "battle with addiction". It's like the language that we use about people who die of cancer and with the same level of fatalism, as if you have lost the challenge already.

What this research does show is that if you use nutrition to help you and you are committed to changing your alcohol habit, you have a very good chance of meeting your goal, way over 50%. Over 80% in both studies had kept their commitment for more than six months. Does that give you confidence? It should. I would take those odds.

The fact that the outcomes for changing alcohol consumption rise exponentially if you get your nutrition right should be shouted from the rooftops. Why isn't it? Instead, you have to be prepared to dig for the information.

When I started researching nutrition, my attitude was: eat whatever and sort out your diet later. This research and lots of other studies that look at behavior and nutrition and depression and nutrition, show me that that approach is wrong. Get your nutrition clear first and embark on your change armed with the right nutritional support in terms of food and supplements.

Now, I am not saying that all is lost if you do not sort out your nutrition at the outset. I certainly didn't but I think I might have felt better much more quickly if I had. I still believe that your priority is to stay away from the first drink so everything else is secondary. But I did not appreciate that caving into the cookies would actually make cravings and mood worse. This is what this chapter is about.

So before you throw out this section as a step too far in the early days, hear me and the research out.

Before we get into exactly what foods you need to be eating, a word about dieting.

Keep it Simple – Eyes on the Prize

It is really tempting to try to attack multiple goals along the lines of "I am going to sort myself out". It's the carpet bombing technique. I suppose the one positive thing you can say about the strategy is that you have to be an optimist to think it will work.

I mentioned earlier in this book, "The One" by Seth Godin. He demonstrates the poor results you get from multi-tasking and emphasizes employing your will power on the one thing.

The other things, you can get to.

Do the other things matter as much?

Go back to the question I asked myself – "what is the thing that I can do which will make the biggest difference to my life? Is the answer the same for you? I suspect that it is.

Succeed one thing at a time. Start with alcohol.

It is a fallacy that multi-tasking makes us more efficient. The opposite is true.

Don't spread your will power too thin. Direct it all at the one thing. Concentrate on one thing at a time.

The point I am arguing here is that if you want things to change, stop frittering away energy and focus and willpower on other things. Do what will give you the biggest pay off and tackle alcohol as a single issue.

If you try to alter your drinking habits while losing weight or going gluten free or vegetarian or paleo or whatever, forget it.

When I decided to stop drinking, I came to that decision because I knew in my bones that giving up drinking was the single thing that would make the most difference in my life. I knew that and there was no argument. Changing other habits was like rearranging the deck chairs on the Titanic. Changing anything else was displacement activity and a possible smoke screen to cover if I did not commit and deliver on what I really needed to do – stop drinking.

So don't widen your vision, narrow it. Do everything that will help you to change your alcohol habit and stop there.

That does not mean that you don't attack the issue from multiple angles. This is about success so use all angles and all weapons available.

Looking at the data on nutrition, we have already established that sorting out your diet and supplementation so it **supports** your alcohol goal would be a very smart move.

Adding raw, vegan, pescatarian, Neanderthal and so on, is unnecessary and will endanger your main goal. Resist the temptation to clean house health-wise.

Eyes on the prize.

If you are reading this, your drinking is worrying you or you know it is holding you back. Concentrate on the one thing you need to do – alter your habits with alcohol.

Where do I start with my diet?

Your framework has to be on non-obsessive, 'healthy' eating.

Many of the approaches out there are based more around fad diets and going to extremes just to shed a few pounds, instead of actually promoting health.

I have a twitter account @3PeasPublishing and one of the things that has struck me is how much revolting looking food is photographed in the name of "Clean Eating".

Clean Eating can be an excellent approach as it means healthy eating, cooking from scratch, no additives. Great!

Clean Eating can also mean no wheat, no dairy, no gluten. And apparently, no plate appeal either.

If you have true allergies or lab tested intolerances, then restricting your diet to exclude foods that you have a reaction to, makes sense. Just cutting out whole sections of food because they are supposedly "unclean" is a distraction from your goal – deal with alcohol.

I will give the most up to date advice on what you need to eat and exclude to support your alcohol goals but as to whether it is clean or not, that is not the focus right now.

If we start with a basically healthy framework, the next thing to consider is how food can prevent relapse.

Now, stopping drinking or cutting down is a process and for many, many people, falling off the wagon or blipping, however you want to term it, is part of the run up with the pole to the high jump or the rocking of the bob sleigh at the start of the slalom. It is part of the process.

But, who knows whether it is necessary? Who knows whether people have multiple attempts because they need to get knocked down and get up again, multiple times or they fall down because the tools to help and the one thing focus has not been given to them?

I don't know the answer but I suggest that if you can avoid the seesaw of off – on – off – on again sobriety, it will save you a lot of anguish.

So, let's understand what you need to do you prevent relapse.

Relapse is preceded by a series of triggers, like little nudges towards the wrong fork on the road. A general, healthy eating program does not take this into account. To bullet proof your nutrition against relapse you need to understand HALT.

The acronym HALT is a where we start. HALT are the triggers, the nudges to watch for:

Hungry

Angry

Lonely

Tired

In a nutritional context, that means that

- You cannot restrict calories too severely or risk triggering the H in Halt.

- You need to build in snacks to avoid hunger building up H

- You need to manage your mood and energy levels to avoid Angry and Tired.

Can nutrition do that? Most certainly it can.

We will talk about sugar and in particular refined sugar in this section. The major point here is that too much sugar amplifies your emotions and fogs your ability to think clearly. So it can contribute to whether you react to something calmly or angrily and the seesaw nature of a sugar high followed by a low most definitely contributes to your feeling tired.

So, although general guidance on nutrition is a good source of advice on how to improve your health, you should concentrate on mood stabilization and energy evenness.

The food and habits to adopt to avoid HALT

In order to avoid the HALT element (hungry-angry-lonely-tired symptoms), you must have a healthy breakfast. Proper nutrition is crucial in fighting all sorts of mental struggles. And it all starts in the morning. Breakfast gives your body something to run on from the get-go and can also sets you on the right course for healthy eating throughout the day. Several studies that examined health practices have confirmed that not eating breakfast is also a risk factor for illness, including overweight. It is also a hangover (pun) from drinking days for many as skipping breakfast is very common with drinkers.

However, just having a bagel and coffee won't do. Sure, this sort of breakfast will give you a rush of energy—but it will cause a drop an hour or so later, when you will probably feel tired, foggy headed, and maybe even grouchy, a bit depressed or at least not as positive about the day as you felt when you were on your coffee high.

Such blood sugar–dependent drama can be prevented by eating a decent, slow release breakfast, one that gives you some protein, some fat, and some starch. That's because a breakfast of all three basic major nutrients can supply you with a steady stream of energy over a period of time and avoid the HALT effect.

When you eat starch, your body immediately breaks this down, giving you energy that lasts about an hour to an hour and a half.

Next, protein, which takes longer to digest, kicks in after about two or two and a half hours.

Finally, fat is converted to energy after three hours.

So a balanced breakfast at 8:00 a.m. can carry you through to lunch.

Both while in recovery and as you're holding to your commitment to abstinence, you need this kind of nutritional support.

Breakfasts

Examples of good breakfasts to avoid HALT are:

Omelette with any filling, except Nutella!

A protein shake - a fruit shake is a bad idea because of the levels of sugar in the volume of fruit. You will definitely get a sugar crash mid-morning.

Chicken sandwich on whole grain bread

Greek style breakfast of feta, olives, humus and whole meal pitta

Smoked mackerel or avocado on whole meal toast

Scrambled eggs with or without smoked salmon, whole wheat toast.

A shop bought sandwich with a fish or meat filling. Discard one of the slices of bread to keep the fast carb load down.

Pancakes with ham and cheese or even a little honey or maple syrup.

A green detox juice - this does not have the protein to sustain you but it puts so little stress on the digestive system that it continues your body's natural overnight detox into the morning and you can actually feel very well on this. A detox juice is based around apple, cucumber, ginger, lemon or lime, lettuce, parsley, kale, chard and spinach. Any combination of these with no more than ½ an apple per serving.

This is a juice not a smoothie, so the fiber is removed leaving juice with vitamins and enzymes naturally occurring. This is why it is gentle on your digestion.

Breakfasts which are not helping you keep your blood sugar steady and therefore risking the H of HALT are:

Porridge, with or without the extra sugar load of the fruit compote. Unless you are using the roughest of steel cut organic oats and full cream milk, this is a fast carb meal which will leave you Hungry by mid-morning

Any breakfast cereals, including muesli. Full of sugar.

Toast unless it is it is made from the type of house brick whole meal bread you get in health food stores and spread with real butter not margarine, or spread with a nut butter.

Baked goods, for example croissant, Danish pastries, donuts, muffins.

Fruit smoothies (unless they have protein added in the form of whey powder, cottage cheese or eggs but still watch the proportion of fruit to everything else. Better to go with no more than 1/3 fruit by volume and add some hydrating vegetables, for example cucumber or lettuce).

Lunches and Suppers

The trick with both meals is to base them around protein and whole vegetables and fruits.

Protein is the macronutrient which builds the body's tissues so having it at every meal ensures that your body is able to rebuild and cope with your new sober life. I will talk later, in the section on mood control, about how import protein is for the messengers in the brain, the neurotransmitters. If you want to elevate your mood and stabilize them, protein at every meal is a must.

Meat protein and some plant protein (avocado, for example) bring with it good fats. Fats are essential for the building of the cell walls and generation of hormones, it is as basic as that. Good fats – olive, avocado, coconut, hemp, flax, fish, walnuts, should not be restricted as they keep your energy levels up without spiking your blood sugar and they give your skin and hair a glow

In terms of animal –v fish –v- plant protein, if you are a vegan or a vegetarian, your decision is made for you. If you eat meat, it is really up to you how you get your protein. Variety is the key.

If you eat fish then a couple of portions of oily fish (salmon, tuna mackerel, swordfish) a week is great for your health. Fish is an anti-inflammatory so it also calms down joint inflammation and helps with skin conditions such as rosacea and eczema.

Plant protein comes in the form of beans, most notably soya and tofu and nuts and seeds.

The jury is out on soya since it was not an ingredient in our diet until relatively recently. It is also an issue for women because of the phyto oestrogens it contains. Phyto estrogens bind to the oestrogen uptake sites in the body so natural oestrogen can be crowded out. This affects fertility and the natural protective properties of eostrogen against osteoporosis.

In menopause, when your own oestrogen drops, it can be helpful for women to have a similar compound binding to oestrogen sites but there is no consensus on whether the lowering of oestrogen in menopause is a natural process that should be left alone, should be treated with synthetic or bio identical hormones or left to phyto estrogens to soften the landing for women.

If you are in your mid to late forties and female, it is worth talking to your GP about the whole oestrogen issue. This is pertinent in recovery as post-menopausal symptoms can include low mood or feelings of being overwhelmed. If you are in recovery, you need to know what to expect and what is menopause and what is recovery and if you are having symptoms which are making recovery very difficult, you may decide that HRT is for you. Alternatively, you may, like me, decide that menopause is a new start and the drop in oestrogen is quite helpful as it brings out the warrior tendencies in women.

There is a reason why post-menopausal women in many cultures are valued as shamans and priestesses.

Nuts and seeds are packed with good things. They are very calorie rich because of the amount of oil they contain but this comes with a mega punch of minerals and trace elements. Measure nuts in small quantities but get a variety is small quantities each week. Peanuts are not nuts at all and should be avoided.

Whichever proteins you eat, make sure you have them at every meal. That will do most to keep your blood sugar steady and that is what you want most of all to support your journey through recovery.

Whole vegetables and fruits supply your carbohydrate, fiber and your micro nutrients – vitamins, minerals and trace elements. Micro nutrients are essential for proper cell functioning and metabolism.

The basics of a healthy diet

The key to a healthy diet lies in eating:

- the right amount of food, taking into consideration how active you are

- a wide variety of foods, comprising fruits and vegetables, rice, bread, pasta, and other starchy foods, with some milk, dairy products, meats and fish and plant proteins such as beans, nuts and seeds.

Ok, let's get real about how your diet may have been. In Food & Behaviour: A Natural Connection" by Barbara Stitt Ph.D., Ms Stitt looked at diet of probationers (yes, prisoners again, only these ones are out) and reported the following patterns:

1. No breakfast

2. High sugar and refined sugar

3. High proportion of processed foods

4. Low protein

5. Low fruit and veg

6. High milk

Apart from the last item, milk, this looks like the gone to hell version of the Eat Well plate or the national diet in Scotland.

Scientists have fed rats with healthy and unhealthy diets and given them access to alcohol. They found that the ones with deficient diets hit the alcohol dropper in their cages more often. (This was a true experience – Beasley and Knightly 1994).

The relative proportions of the macro nutrients are: 45 percent carbohydrate, 30 percent fat and 25 percent protein. That is a starting point for a healthy diet.

You may want to increase your protein if you are very active in weight-bearing sports, or increase your carbs if you run, play tennis or are doing anything endurance-related. You also need to monitor your mood. Some people do well on a high protein diet, others feel like zombies. Others are very moody on too much carb. So take this guide as a starting point and work out what is right for you.

There has been a recent focus on "paleo" diet. This diet is a form of natural, low carbohydrate diet where your plate is made up of the sort of food you would eat when we were all cavemen. It sounds bizarre but the idea is that our bodies are not too evolved from that time that we can cope with grains in particular. To feel well and manage our weight, we should go back to what we ate four thousand years ago – meat, plants, a few berries. No dairy, no grains.

For you as a former heavy drinker, this diet is not bad but be careful that this does not become an ultra-low carbohydrate level in this diet. We all need some carb to give us energy and help with serotonin levels in the brain (see later in this book).

More about sugar in the next section.

How does eating the right foods help?

Your goal is to support your body as it begins to clear itself of alcohol and to help avoid cravings or switch them off, if they strike.

In the early stages, the first six months, food can help rebuild your metabolic processes, rest and recuperate your organs and stabilize your moods and energy levels.

It can also help with one of the most likely effects of not drinking, insomnia.

Sleep is important because traditional Chinese medicine tells us that the liver does most of its repair work between 1am and 3am. Adrenal repair also happens at night and the digestive system is eliminating toxins at night.

Where are you starting from?

Understand your starting point from drinking- How is alcohol metabolised and how does withdrawal work?

Our bodies don't store alcohol. It is processed and removed from our bodies by our livers. How does this process work? When you drink alcohol, some of it is absorbed by your stomach, and some of it goes to your bloodstream. But most of the alcohol is absorbed in the small intestine. The part that goes into your bloodstream travels to all parts of your body. It also ends up in your liver where it is broken down by enzyme called alcohol dehydrogenase (ADH). It is then decomposed to acetaldehyde, and finally to carbon.

Now what exactly happens when you stop drinking?

First, if you are intending to go cold turkey, get your doctor's advice first. I am not being dramatic when I say that alcohol withdrawal can be life threatening. But bear in mind that many doctors are drinkers so they may play down your concerns with your drinking and even try to put you off stopping. Sad but true.

Having got yourself ready for withdrawal, you put down your last glass. In the first 72 hours your body is cleaning itself from all the remaining alcohol in your system. Some usual symptoms which happen after about 6 hours of the last drink are: high temperature and blood pressure, rapid pulse, sweating, anxiety, insomnia, etc. As I said, it can be more serious. Some people, however, lose consciousness. Full detoxification will take about two weeks.

After that, the alcohol is out and recovery can begin. My recollection is of elation and relief that I was a non-drinker. When you pass the two week period, you will start noticing some amazing changes and benefits of your decision.

If you have been drinking for any period of time, you have probably not looked after yourself terribly well in nutritional terms.

Your body will be depleted of vitamins and minerals; you may have blood sugar instability and low mood. You may be a bit overweight, you might have dry skin, or drinker's glow in your cheeks.

The body you have inherited post alcohol needs some help but moods even more so.

The fact that you are not drinking will be a massive help as the body can do a lot to repair itself, if you give it a chance. Good nutrition is in part, the fuel for the body to do the healing for you.

The good news is that nutrition can help you rebuild and surpass the health you had before you started on your drinking path. This should not just be a vague: "it would be nice to look and feel better". Having gone into recovery from alcohol issues, you deserve to feel the best you can so you can really capitalise on your AFness. You should be jumping for joy about being free but you need the energy and vitality to do that.

You probably don't feel like that at the moment. Alcohol is very likely to have led to you not eating properly. Alcohol limits the appetite, so heavy drinkers eat less real food and take more empty calories from alcohol.

If you have been drinking hazardously for any amount of time, from months to years, you will have set up a nutritional plan which looks like this: 50% or more of your calories in the form of alcohol. The remaining calories will be from junk food or an attempt at a healthy diet but you cannot outrun the fact that excessive alcohol is sugar without nutrition.

Alcohol provides a lot of energy without nutrients so the energy provided is short-term and leaves the body without proper nutritional stores to draw on. The alcohol gives you a sugar high followed by a drop in blood sugar. You have been existing with a see-saw effect on your blood sugar.

If you drove your car going between pedal to the metal and hard on the brake, your car would not last long and the wear and tear on the engine would be huge. Think of that in your body.

What can I do to get my nutrition to support my no alcohol/low alcohol goals?

Just removing the alcohol and starting to eat real food, is going to make you feel better.

You may have terrible energy lows in the afternoon, barely able to make it between 3 and 6pm. This might have been the hangover kicking in and you would probably have fixed it with an evening drink.

When you stop drinking, you lose the drinking – hangover cycle and you should not feel dreadful mid to late afternoon. But you will if you are continuing to chuck sugar at your diet.

If you follow the advice in this chapter, you will see the following benefits:

- stable energy levels and mood

- less feelings of aggression, overwhelm or tearfulness

- less mental fog

- better skin, you get the glow on the outside to match your recovery on the inside

- If you suffer from thrush, fewer or no attacks

The elephant in the room is that you are not starting from the same starting line as a non-drinker. So general healthy eating advice is not enough.

Moods is a massive issue both in terms of the risk they pose of relapse and because they are a miserable way to get started as a sober person. Alcohol is a depressant plus many of us drank to medicate depression.

When the brain is getting all it needs nutritionally and there are no alcohol or drugs or caffeine interfering or taxing the brain, the brain is making neurotransmitters using our nutrition. These neurotransmitters, mainly made from protein, regulate many things, including our moods and behavior.

If there are imbalances in neurotransmitters through poor diet or the disruption that alcohol creates, this will affect your mood and behaviour and trigger cravings.

So, what you eat can help or make it much harder to stay away?

A general' healthy eating programme is not going to cut it. It does not prioritise brain processes to help mood or the extra help you need to repair organs that have been coping with too much alcohol.

Food to support your emotional balance

Apart from cravings, and we have looked at nutrition to help you avoid those, the thing that most drinkers worry about most is how they will cope of they don't have their friend alcohol. They see alcohol as helping them calm down, relax, pep up, be happy, and be creative. Fill in the links for your own story.

If you kick the crutch away, how will you cope? Well first, no-one died of an emotion. If you feel a bit flat or even low, there are plenty of better ways to elevate your mood, exercise being the obvious one.

But this section is about nutrition. Can nutrition elevate your mood? Yes. The neurotransmitters in your brain are responsible for mood and behavior. If those are functioning well and in balance, you will feel well. Indeed, you will feel far better than when you drank.

One of the lies of alcohol is that it makes you feel better. It does not. What it does do is correct the mess you feel as a result of your last drinking session. Alcohol disrupts your balance so your mood and energy levels are out of whack. The result is that you feel awful and hey presto! A drink makes you feel better. But, all the drink is doing is making you feel approaching normal. If you take the alcohol away and give your body the nutritional support you need to recover, you won't get the lows in the first place.

The "high" from a drink is how you should feel most of the time as a healthy person. When your brain chemicals are really out of whack, your alcohol withdrawal feels more like flu or upset stomach or arthritis. You have joint pains, loose stools, headache, fogginess and memory loss.

So, how do you rebuild your emotional balance? There are four groups of brain chemicals that need to get back into balance: serotonin, endorphins, GABA and dopamine and the other catecholines.

- **Serotonin**

Serotonin is the brain chemical that regulates your mood, sleep, pain, emotion and appetite, it also influences self-control, impulse control (we need that one) and the ability to plan ahead.

Low serotonin also leads to sugar cravings and caffeine cravings – anything to pick yourself up.

Research from 2010 by Gant and Lewis proves the link between simple carbohydrate and the release or serotonin in the brain.

So, if you have been drinking excessively and therefore taking in a lot of sugar, you will have been stimulating serotonin, over stimulating it and you get to the point where the brain turns off more production of serotonin. When you stop drinking and thereby tipping sugar into your system, your serotonin drops and you feel low.

I think it helps even just to understand why you are feeling low and that it is fixable but may take a little time.

These chemicals help with pain and stress and help you feel good. These are the feel good chemicals released with prolonged exercise.

- **Endorphins**

  As with Serotonin, alcohol disrupts the metabolism of this chemical and binds to the site where endorphins should bind. The body thinks you have enough endorphins and switches production off.

  When you stop drinking, alcohol comes out of the body and the endorphin sites are bare. You feel low and you crave things that will give you a rush, particularly sugar. Without endorphins you can feel overwhelmed and teary.

  There is one other effect of low endorphin levels, lowered immunity (research from 2008 by Cowen). The immune cells in our body have endorphin sites. These cells can't function properly without them. The result is that you are prone to infection, viruses, and cancer and auto immune diseases. Happy days

- **GABA**

GABA is a relaxation chemical in the brain. Mental relaxation rather than emotional relaxation (Serotonin does this job). It is described as natural valium. If you used alcohol to relax, perhaps medicating with alcohol for anxiety, low production of GABBA is something to watch out for.

- **Dopamine and other Catecholamines**

These chemicals are energizing. You need them for focus and alertness.

- **Recovery foods for neurotransmitters**

So, having gone through the chemicals in the brain which most affect mood and emotional wellbeing and pretty much shown that alcohol will have messed them up.

What can we do to get balance back as quickly as possible when you take alcohol out of your system?

The first point is that all the neurotransmitters we have discussed are made of protein. So you need to be eating enough protein.

Next, you need to take out of your diet any other chemicals which are messing up your neural balance – principally, nicotine, sugar and caffeine. Sorry but true.

Third, you need to make sure that you are ingesting the right fats, Omega 3s.

Some specific steps you can take to target particular neurotransmitters:

Serotonin – make sure you have enough Tryptophan in your diet. So eggs, turkey sesame and sunflower seeds, kelp, bananas, almonds, pork, shrimp, wild game, chicken, tempeh and milk. Make sure you have some carbohydrate with these foods as you need the carbohydrate to transport the Tryptophan across the blood brain pathway.

Try St John's Wort which increases Serotonin activity

Get enough light and use full spectrum bulbs to mimic the sun.

- **Blood sugar and hypoglycemia**

This is very likely to be something that you need to address.

The good news is diet is the solution.

Hypoglycemia means low blood sugar, often in reaction to a release of sugar in the blood from food eaten. If you eat a lot of sugar, you set up a see saw effect with sugar hitting the blood, the body trying to regulate this by removing sugar and creating hypoglycemia.

Hypoglycemia is not a good state to be in because it leads to energy and mood swings. It taxes your pancreas where insulin spikes, risks type 2 diabetes and it taxes your adrenal glands because adrenaline is also produced when blood glucose levels drop. You can get the shakes, weakness, sweats and rapid heartbeat.

Alcohol is not the only thing that causes hypoglycemia, caffeine and a high sugar diet are up there too.

If you do this for long enough, the body will just break .and you get what is called Adrenal Fatigue (see later).

In a prison study in 2004 (Stitt) (prisoners are great addiction subject because, provided they are on lock down, they are going to go cold turkey on whatever substances they have been taking) showed that 85% were hypoglycemic.

- **Recovery foods from hypoglycemia**

The solution to this is completely within your reach through nutrition. If you have been eating irregularly because of alcohol, now you need to get a grip and get a set eating pattern; three meals a day plus snacks.

Simple carbohydrates, so sugar and refined carbohydrates are no nos. Protein and fats should be in every meal and snack. No skipping meals.

- **Which foods to avoid**

All junk, and sugar (including fruit on its own and particularly exotic fruit).

- **Adrenal fatigue**

When adrenal fatigue starts to occur, your adrenal glands slow down, they are slow to react to low blood sugar. The adrenals also release adrenaline to tell the body to take sugar out of the blood. So slow adrenals have serious side effects.

Your see saw of blood sugar becomes more pronounced, and you feel tired, sleepy, confused, angry, weepy, anxious and you have memory loss.

The classic symptom of adrenal fatigue is if you sit down for even a few minutes and fall asleep. Adrenal fatigue also shows itself in over reaction to things.

- **Recovery foods for adrenal fatigue**

The first thing to do is to stabilize your blood sugar levels. With regular meals based around protein and fat. Lots of vegetables and no junk.

- **Allergies and sensitivities**

You may think that we are straying into bunkum territory here but if you accept that you drank for the pay off, sometimes the payoff is the rush you get from an allergic reaction.

In conversation with the Three Peas nutritionist (Three Peas publish this book and have a health and fitness website at www.threepeaspublishing.com), she is clear that one of the results of an allergy is that if you eat the food, the body treats it as a toxin and releases psychoactive chemicals which give you a high. Often, the foods that people are most allergic to are the ones they crave because of the physical reaction, the internal high they cause.

If you accept that the sort of person who drinks excessively is the sort of person who is used to living a high-low see saw existence in terms of the things that they ingest, then it should be no surprise that research on alcoholics shows much higher than average incidence of allergies. If you want to check out the facts, and we are back to prisoners again, "End Your Addiction Now" by

Dr. Charles Gant includes a prison study. Dr. Gant was the psychiatric consultant for New York State Prison.

The allergies we are talking about can be to food and environment (gas, paints, perfumes plastics, disinfectants). The food allergies can be almost anything. I had myself tested and I am allergic to egg white, coconut, lemon and cashews with lesser reactions to other foods. I thought it was bunkum until I realized that the ice-cream alternative that I had become "addicted" to, called BoojaBooja, is made with, wait for it, cashews, coconut and cocoa. I had developed a rash, which I had thought stress-induced. I know I can be pig-headed but I stopped with the ice cream and within three or four hours, the rash, which had been around for about 8 weeks, stopped. That convinced me.

For drinkers, the allergy can often be alcohol related so grapes, grape skins, wheat, barley and sugars.

This is something you should check out, particularly if you find yourself in sobriety or moderation craving foods. You will probably know yourself why you crave them and if it is because they cause a physical effect, like a high or spacing out, they must be avoided. You did not come off alcohol or dial it back to simply to recreate the effect with something else. You came off alcohol or dialed it back to be fully present and reach your potential as a human being.

Leaky gut

Leaky gut is when spaces in the gut wall develop and pieces of food can pass into the blood stream. Toxins can also pass. You get an auto-immune response and symptoms such as bloating, gas and allergies.

If you suspect that you have been eating foods to which you are allergic for months or years, or if you are having IBS type symptoms, you can think about a nutritional program specifically for leaky gut.

The best I know is "10 Years Younger in 10 Weeks" by Thorborg Hafsteinsdottir. You can get it on Amazon paper and eBook.

She includes in her book, a cleanse and rebuild programme for your gut, which includes specific supplements for leaky gut. The book is quite radical in the no junk, no chemicals, my body is a temple way of thinking but if you are plagued with bloating or feel really under par, this is a good programme for rebuilding yourself, Navy Seal style.

Thrush/candida

Thrush is very common in heavy drinkers. I didn't know that. Thrush is an imbalance of bacteria so the good bacteria are not keeping the bad bacteria under control. Bad diet is a contributor so lots of refined carbohydrate is the culprit yet again. When the candida bacteria digests sugar, it produces alcohol and it grows. Like little Gremlins, the more candida you have, the more carbohydrates they need and the more you crave carbohydrates.

The top three pieces of advice to get thrush under control are:

1. Take sugar out of your diet. Starve the buggers.

2. Add good bacteria back in. You can get oral capsules of good bacteria called Lactobacillus Acidophilus at your local health food store. Just make sure that it is sold refrigerated and you keep it in the fridge until you use it.

3. Help your good bacteria with a good diet of fresh vegetables and make sure you are using natural antiseptics like garlic, calendula, turmeric and some antifungal foods such as avocado, lemon, kale, olive oil and onion.

Avoid fruit, dried fruit and fruit juices, vinegars, mushrooms, malts, soy, pickles and processed meats. cheese, peanuts

Add supplements that fight yeasts: citrus seed extract, caprylic acid, kyolic garlic extract.

One other tip is to exercise, particularly yoga, trampoline or rebounder. The reason is that your lymph system will flush out bacteria. The twists in yoga and the bouncing in trampoline help the lymph system get moving.

Nutritional deficiencies

- Protein particularly the amino acid Tyrosine is needed to rebuild. As we discussed in the nutrition chapter, protein is also very important for keeping blood sugar stable.

- Fats. Stick to oils found in nuts, seeds and fish. For Omega 3, used flax seed oil and fish oil.

- Stay away from processed oils such as hydrogenated and partially hydrogenated oils. And oils in fried food.

- Most common deficiencies are Vitamin A, Thiamine, Riboflavin, Panthonenic Acid and B6

- Chromium regulates blood sugar. If you are hypoglycemic, as you are likely to be, chromium is important to stabilize blood sugar.

- Zinc helps with liver function, immunity and brain function. Excessive sugar, alcohol, caffeine and drugs depletes zinc.

- Calcium and magnesium. Alcohol depletes calcium and caffeine more so. Magnesium is a calmer and a relaxer but alcohol depletes it.

- Iron. If your liver is damaged, it prevents you from absorbing iron. To help digestion of iron, you need to make sure you are having your omega 3 fats, copper, Vitamin B complex and Vitamin C.

- Potassium. Low potassium can cause heart disease and high blood pressure. Alcohol and caffeine deplete potassium.

- Vitamin C is a detoxifier. Because it is water soluble, your body cannot store it so you need to keep up a regular supply.

Chapter 6

Supplements

The first point to make is that your aim should be to get all the nutrients you need from your food. Supplements are a last resort.

Second point is that self-medication is dangerous.

So, if you live in a country with a government health service, ask for some tests to look at your levels of key vitamins and minerals. If you live in a pay or you die country, you will need to pay for tests.

If you can't bring yourself to see a specialist, limit your pill popping to a good multivitamin, a B Complex and Vitamin C.

Also, think about what is driving you to want to take lots of supplements. Is that urge healthy at all?

Look at this quote from Potatoes not Prozac by Kathleen DesMaisons:

People with addictive bodies love to take something, be it pills, white powder or special mixtures in a can. Taking something becomes the solution rather than creating a lifestyle with a healthy relationship with food. Eating food is your solution to sugar sensitivity or addiction demands that you think about what food you will eat, how and with whom"

I agree with this absolutely. In relation to the last point, about eating with others, one of the things that food can give you once you don't depend on alcohol, is a way to connect with people. Remember, the opposite of addiction is connection.

Adding supplements is an emergency measure to help your body recover.

Subject to expert advice and tests for your own needs, what follows are some general comments on the sorts of supplements that may be recommended for you:

In this stage of recovery, certain food supplements can play a major role in helping you resist cravings or rebuild your looks. You are still in early recovery and your body has been starved of real food and has had the assault of ethanol, as a toxin. Your organs have been overly axed by ethanol and you have probably not had enough rest or proper sleep while drinking heavily.

So, supplements are very helpful in helping the body to help itself.

B Complex

One of the most important groups of vitamins for helping to rebuild alcohol damage to the body is definitely Vitamin B. A lot of people who consume, or used to consume alcohol are deficient in B vitamins. B vitamins are helpful for energy levels so a B-complex can help with the tiredness that drinkers often feel in the first three months of sobriety.

Vitamin B3 is sometimes used intravenously to help people stop drinking alcohol. If this is not your case, a nutritionist will probably recommend 100mg of B-complex per day.

Supplementing with vitamin B1 (thiamine) is essential for ensuring proper brain function and decreasing fatigue, brain fog and poor memory. Wernickie-Korsakoff syndrome, or alcoholic encephalopathy (wet brain), is a pronounced form of thiamin deficiency.

Research has shown that vitamin B3, or niacin, helps heavy drinkers detox from alcohol and wards off wet brain. Even if you are still drinking, B3 is worth taking.

Vitamin B5, or pantothenic acid, helps support adrenal function and also helps rid the body of alcohol. So B5 also helps with adrenal exhaustion and blood sugar regulation.

If you are struggling to get to sleep or stay asleep or feel anxious vitamin B6, pyridoxine, is crucial for the production of serotonin and melatonin.

Vitamin C is the other vitamin that is almost always recommended because it supports detox and will have been depleted because of your drinking. Since Vitamin C is water soluble, anything that your body cannot use, is washed out in your urine so you do not need to worry about overdose.

Other more specialist supplements

Some heavy drinkers are deficient in the substance called prostaglandin E1 (PGE1) and in gamma-linolenic acid (GLA).

4 grams per day of evening primrose oil will fix this. It contains about 360 mg of GLA.

If you are taking evening primrose, it is very high in a particular fatty acid that needs to be balanced out in the body by other omegas. The point is to make sure you are eating oily fish at least twice a week if you are taking evening primrose.

For relaxation, you can take a magnesium citrate supplement. 600mg per day. This is a muscle relaxant, which is why you can also buy magnesium salts as a bath soak (Epsom salts). Magnesium citrate will help you feel less overwhelmed if you have a tendency to catastrophize. Take this for a month. Have Epsom Salts baths a couple of times a week, soaking in a good cupful in a hot bath for at least twenty minutes. This is especially just before bed.

A supplement specific to liver is Milk Thistle. Pharmacists recommend Milk Thistle to be taken while you are drinking, the morning after to help the liver do its detox function. Milk Thistle has the unique ability to help regenerate damaged liver cells.

It is particularly useful for increasing production of glutathione—a powerful antioxidant produced by the body, as well as increasing the levels of other antioxidants, such as superoxide dismutase.

The active ingredient in Milk Thistle, Silymarin has the unique ability to regenerate liver cells. By acting as a blocker, Silymarin not only helps maintain liver health, but slows the progression of irreversible liver damage, also known as cirrhosis.

The dosage is usually 420mg per day split into three doses.

One thing to be aware of with Milk Thistle is that is a powerful detoxifier. If you are going to take it, you should have at least a month of healthy eating first. The reason is that the body will detox naturally if you are eating a good diet. That detox will happen naturally with cells releasing their waste into the blood and lymph systems gradually so as not to overwhelm systems. If you introduce Milk Thistle too early, the body will have too many toxins to deal with at one time and they will get dumped back into the blood stream again to be taken up by cells all over again.

If you are going to do anything approaching a detox or a juice "reboot" in the first year of sobriety, choose a well-structured programme which runs over several weeks with a wind up, full detox and wind down process built in. Milk Thistle should only be taken in the middle to late part of a detox after the body has already processed the low hanging fruit in terms of toxins.

Chapter 7

Foods that Target the Liver and Recipes

Liver supporting foods and recipes

There are some foods that are perfect for your liver.

1. Artichokes

Various studies have shown that regular intake of artichokes lowers fat and cholesterol levels in your liver.

2. Avocado

Avocado is one of the best foods for your liver. Avocado contains vitamins C and E, which are strong antioxidants and effectively neutralize free radicals, thereby protecting the liver cells against damage. Avocado is also anti-fungal, so good for fighting thrush.

Carrot

Carrot is another great, liver supporting vegetable. It is rich with precious beta-carotene, flavonoids and proteins that will improve liver function

Citrus fruits

Orange, lemon, lime, grapefruits...eat, drink and enjoy. These fruits are extremely healthy for your liver and they are anti-bacterial so help to maintain gut health.

Garlic

No matter how you use it, garlic will definitely help your liver by activating certain enzymes that promote the toxin removal. It is also very rich in vitamin B6 and vitamin C. Garlic is an antiseptic so it assists gut health and fights thrush.

3. Green vegetables

Green vegetables have an amazing effect on your liver.

Broccoli is the detox king of vegetables. Broccoli has a strong, positive impact on our body's detoxification system. Researchers have recently identified one of the key reasons for this detox benefit: Glucoraphanin, gluconasturtiian, and glucobrassicin are 3 glucosinolate phytonutrients found in a special combination in broccoli. This dynamic trio is able to support all steps in the body's detox process, including activation, neutralization, and elimination of unwanted contaminants. Isothiocyanates (ITCs) are the detox-regulating molecules made from broccoli's glucosinolates, and they help control the detox process at a genetic level. Serve it fresh as a side dish, or a salad or stir fry it with coconut oil and almonds. You can't beat it.

5. Tomato

Tomatoes are very rich in vitamin C and folic acid, but its most powerful ingredient is certainly lycopene - the red pigment which is extremely rich in antioxidants that literally heal your liver. Unlike other fruits and vegetables, tomatoes are more nutritious cooked at cooking activates the lycopene.

8. Walnuts

Walnuts are rich in important amino acids, and they help the liver in detoxification of harmful substances, especially ammonia.

Love Your Liver recipes

1. Moroccan Sunshine Salad

I like this salad because it reminds me of North African holidays. It is just really fabulous, sun shiny food.

Ingredients:

2 cups of lettuce, chopped

1 large orange

¼ cup of walnuts

¼ cup of dates, finely chopped

1 tbsp of fresh lemon juice

Preparation:

Combine the ingredients in a large bowl and season with lemon juice. Mix well and serve cold.

2. Baked Eggs with Roast Avocado

This is a nice twist on baked eggs but using the avocado shells to house the potatoes. Eggs and avocado are is nutritional gold.

Ingredients:

3 medium ripe avocados, cut in half

6 eggs

1 medium tomato, finely chopped

3 tbsp of olive oil

2 tsp of dried rosemary

Salt and pepper to taste

Preparation:

Preheat oven to 350 degrees. Cut avocado in half and remove the flesh from the center. Place one egg and chopped tomato in each avocado half and sprinkle with rosemary, salt and pepper. Grease the baking pan with olive oil and place the avocados. You want to use a small baking pan so your avocados can fit tightly. Place in the oven for about 15-20 minutes. Serve with sliced avocado.

3. Spinach pancakes

This recipe calls for cottage cheese or ricotta. Ricotta is more correct in combination with the spinach but cottage cheese is a lighter option.

I have chosen to use coconut oil for this recipe because it is the only oil which it is safe to heat to a smoking temperature. Every other oil will start converting to trans-fat when you heat it on high.

Ingredients:

1 cup of all-purpose flour

2 eggs

½ tsp of salt

1 tbsp of sour cream or crème fraiche

2 tsp of baking powder

1 cup of milk

1 cup of cottage cheese or Ricotta

1 cup of spinach, cooked and drained

2 tsp coconut oil

Preparation:

Combine the flour, eggs, salt, sour cream, baking powder, and 1 cup of milk in a bowl. Mix well with an electric mixer until nice and smooth mixture. If you don't have a mixer, you can beat this by hand.

Cover the mixture and let it stand for 15 minutes.

In another bowl, mix the cottage cheese or Ricotta with the drained spinach. Beat well with a fork. Set aside.

Put the coconut oil in a frying pan and heat until it smokes… Use ¼ cup of mixture to make one thin pancake. Fry your pancakes for about 10-15 seconds on each side. This mixture should give you 6 pancakes.

Spread 1 tbsp of cheese mixture over each pancake and serve.

4. Greek Salad with Tuna

Ingredients:

1 small onion, chopped

1 iceberg lettuce or two Romaine hearts

2 medium ripe red tomatoes, chopped

½ cup fresh cilantro, chopped

2 cups of oil-free tuna, drained or fresh tuna

1 lime, juiced

4 ounces of feta cheese, chopped into bite size pieces

Salt to taste

2 tbsp of low fat sour cream or Greek yoghurt

Preparation:

Combine the tomatoes, onions, cilantro and lettuce in a mixing bowl. Add the lime juice and tuna. If you are using fresh tuna, sear it in a very hot pan for no more than two minutes of each side. Gently toss to evenly distribute the ingredients and transfer into serving bowls. Serve with some Feta and sour cream on top.

6. Protein Explosion Salad

Ingredients:

1 piece of turkey breast, boneless and skinless

2 eggs

1 cup of red cabbage, grated

1 medium tomato

½ cup of olives

1 cup of scallions, chopped

Few artichokes

Few pieces of baby corn

2 tbsp of olive oil

2 tbsp of vegetable oil

Salt to taste

1 tbsp of fresh lemon juice

Preparation:

Wash and pat dry the meat with a kitchen paper. Cut into 1 inch thick strips. In a large skillet, heat up the vegetable oil. Fry the turkey strips for about 10 minutes. Remove from the heat and soak the excess oil with a kitchen paper. Transfer to a large bowl.

Meanwhile boil the eggs for about 7-8 minutes. Remove from the heat, drain and peel. Cut into slices.

Add the remaining ingredients into the bowl and mix well. Add salt to taste and fresh lemon juice.

Juices for sobriety

You will need a juicer for this. I am afraid that you get what you pay for. The best and most expensive juicers re "centrifugal" so they spin round very fast and use centrifugal force to pulse the food through fine sieve-like appliance and get the juice out the other end.

My own juicer is the Sage by Heston Blumenthal. It is powerful, fast and easy to clean. The feeder tube is wide enough to take whole lettuce hearts and apples. Almost all the parts are dishwasher safe, apart from the lid which for some inexplicable reason, you need to hand wash. The filter needs a good scrub each time and that is not a job for a dish washer. Time to wash up after making a juice, 5 minutes max. Job done.

I also have a traditional jug blender and a Nutri Bullet. I tend to use the Nutribullet as it is quicker and less cumbersome to clean as the blender jug is heavy glass. I have the professional Nutribullet only because it has a bigger capacity so I can make smoothies for more than one person in one go. If I need larger quantities, I use my blender. The entry level priced Nutribullet cup is tiny so I would not recommend getting that.

The aim in the morning is a big and I mean big glass of smoothie or juice to really get the nutrients in first thing.

I do not advise making up these juices and sitting them in the fridge overnight. All juices are best drunk immediately. Some of the juices will keep without tasting very different, the tomato juice for example, but I still think it is best to have them straight away. If you need to save time in the morning, measure out the amount of all ingredients and have it pre- packed ingredient by ingredient ready to pop into the juicer or blender, cookery programme style.

I always start my day with a green juice. This sets me up and so whatever I am doing during the day, I have started the day right nutritionally. It is part of my Morning Ritual.

1. Green Juice

My green juice will have a base of some green leaves – spinach, kale, lettuce, parsley, watercress plus whatever else I have in the fridge which is green – cucumber, peppers and courgettes. I like cucumber in particular as its astringency makes me feel really well in the morning. Parsley is a good digestive so if you are feeing at all "green", add some parsley. To cut the green taste a little I use a lime but you can also use a lemon in you like. The final ingredient is an apple for sweetness. Juice and enjoy and your body will thank you.

Ingredients

1 Romaine heart or Cos lettuce

3 handfuls of spinach leaves, kale, flat leaf parsley or watercress

1 whole cucumber

1 lime or 1 small lemon

1 small red/pink apple

Ice

Preparation:

Put your juicer on low and feed in the lettuce or alternatives, then the cucumber. Turn your juicer to high and whizz the lime/lemon and apple.

Stir together and drink immediately.

If you are taking any morning supplements, take them now.

2. Tomato juice

This tomato juice is nice first thing and the colour is a real wake up. If you want to give it extra kick you can add Tabasco to make it more like a Virgin Mary.

Ingredients:

1 glass of water (you can use tonic instead)

1 pound of fresh tomatoes

5 carrots

1 t5 tbsp of brown sugar or sugar substitute (coconut nectar, agave or xylitol)

Ice

Preparation:

Wash the vegetables.

Put your juicer on high and pass the carrots through first. Turn your juicer to low and add the tomatoes. Remove the jug from the juicer and whisk in the sugar/sugar substitute.

This one can be kept in the fridge for up to 24 hours. Mix with other ingredients in a blender and keep in the refrigerator.

3. **Super Love Your Liver juice**

The broccoli is the main event in this juice. Broccoli is the king of detox vegetables. Broccoli is hard to digest in its whole state raw but as a juice, all the detox supporting phytonutrients are extracted ready to be absorbed with minimal stress on your digestive system.

Mint is great for digestion. Did you know that animals seek out mint in the wild when they have a stomach ache?

This is heavy on equipment using both a juicer and a blender

The addition of yoghurt and honey in this recipe makes this more of a smoothie than a juice. If you are not keen on smoothies, just leave out the last smoothie stage and drink this as a juice

Ingredients:

1 cup of chopped broccoli

Half bunch of fresh spinach

½ cup of low fat yogurt

1 tsp of honey

Few leaves of mint

¼ cup of water

Ice

Preparation:

Wash the vegetables and put into the juicer on low. Put some ice cubes and blend together until smooth mixture.

4. Berry Blast Juice

I have talked about the importance of berries because of their antioxidant properties, their lack of impact on your blood sugar and their ability to satisfy your need for something sweet when you have an alcohol craving.

This morning smoothie can be made with whatever berries you have available. If you are using frozen berries, don't try to juice them as you will get slush. Just put them in the blender. Spinach can be juiced or blended. To save you using multiple equipment that needs to be cleaned go with one regimen or the other.

Ingredients:

1 cup of mixed blueberries, raspberries, blackberries and strawberries

½ cup of chopped baby spinach

1.5 glass of water

Ice

Preparation:

Wash the baby spinach and put it in a blender. Add other ingredients and mix well for about 30 seconds. Serve cold.

5. Pink Fizz

This shake has the benefit of high quality protein and minerals from the walnuts. Melon is also a great diuretic so if you are feeling puffy, this is a good choice. Cinnamon is a brilliant spice for supporting detox.

Ingredients:

¼ cup of fresh strawberries

¼ of banana

1 slice of melon

½ tsp of cinnamon

¼ cup of chopped walnuts

1 tsp of brown sugar or sugar substitute (coconut nectar, agave or xylitol

Ice

Preparation:

Mix ingredients in a blender and sprinkle with cinnamon. Drink immediately or keep in the refrigerator and serve cold.

6. Strawberry Shake US style

This is a pretty simple milkshake recipe. The main event is the strawberries and their phyto nutrients. If you want to make this a meal replacement, just add some flavoured or plain whey protein, one scoop.

Ingredients:

1 cup of strawberries

½ cup of skim milk

1 tsp of agave syrup

Preparation:

Mix the ingredients in a blender for few minutes. Leave it in the refrigerator for few minutes and serve cold. You can add some ice cubes in it.

7. Rocket fuel

Goji berries are the most nutritionally dense fruit on Earth.

Unique among fruits because they contain all essential amino acids, goji berries also have the highest concentration of protein of any fruit. They are also loaded with vitamin C, contain more carotenoids than any other food, have twenty-one trace minerals, and are high in fiber. Boasting 15 times the amount of iron found in spinach, as well as calcium, zinc, selenium and many other important trace minerals, there is no doubt that the humble goji berry is a nutritional powerhouse.

This amazing little super fruit also contains natural anti-inflammatory, anti-bacterial and anti-fungal compounds. Their powerful antioxidant properties and polysaccharides help to boost the immune system. It's no wonder then, that in traditional Chinese medicine they are renowned for increasing strength and longevity.

This juice also has broccoli so this really is rocket fuel for your liver.

Ingredients:

1 cup of fresh broccoli

1 glass of water

1 cup of goji berries

1 tbsp of brown sugar or sugar substitute (coconut nectar, agave or xylitol)

Preparation:

Put the broccoli in a juicer. Mix the juice with other ingredients in a blender for 30 seconds and serve cold.

That is the end of the recipes.

The legal bit is next and then I have some concluding thoughts about sobriety 18 months on, details of how to download my free, bonus books and also news of the rest of my series:

Disclaimer

designed for an average healthy man and woman who has no health problems. Before using this book, be sure to consult a doctor. In no event shall the author be liable for any direct, indirect, incidental, punitive, or consequential damages of any kind whatsoever with respect to the service, the materials and the products contained within. This eBook is not a substitute for professional nutritional or health advice.

Bonus books

The first is one of my publisher's books in the Weight Loss Clinic series. I think it is very relevant for you because it is called "Sweet Treat" and it is all about desserts which do not use sugar.

So, having read this book, you know that sugar will make achieving your goal that much harder. This book gives you some ideas if you really want something sweet. Plus it's free.

In it you will find recipes for desserts: from Chocolate Thins and Berry Frozen Yoghurt to Grilled Pears and Ricotta.

You can download this at www.threepeaspublishing.com/eatingcleanbutkeepitleansweettr eat

My second free book is the eBook original edition of "Alcohol Free Drinks". I talk about that book in just a minute as the paperback version second edition is on Amazon.

Other books by me

I have three other books that are also about aspects of going alcohol free or alcohol moderate.

One is an Amazon Best Seller.

It is called

Alcohol: Top Ten Cravings Busters

It does what it says on the tin – so it explains what cravings are and then goes through the top ten ways to avoid cravings or switch them off.

I wrote it to help people as one of the main things that I think stops people stopping is fear of cravings.

It is available on Amazon and here is the quick link

http://tinyurl.com/hcf8dgz

Here is what reviewers have very kindly said:

All Five Stars.

Great for beginners
By marion on 10 April 2016
Format: Kindle Edition Verified Purchase
Some very useful tips for managing cravings especially in the early days of sobriety. She does include people who want to moderate their drinking as well as those who want to give up altogether.

By A Customer on 12 April 2016
Format: Kindle Edition Verified Purchase
Really found this easy to read and didn't make me feel as though I was a lost cause!! A lot of other 'Alcohol' related books have made me feel like a loser and that there is no way out. The advice is to the point with some really helpful advice and tips

By The_Urban_Muse on 11 May 2016
Format: Kindle Edition Verified Purchase
This is short, punchy and humorous. I tend to get bored with the repetitive books; they seem to infer that they act as some sort of subliminal message (almost hypnotic), but I can't get into them, as I keep thinking that I've already read that bit!
Neither does the author dwell anyone's morose past, with alcohol induced tales of woe (I do enjoy reading these books too, as I'm a nosy old bat!).
Ultimately it is down to the individual, as no one can wave a magic

wand, and you will be, "Cured!" It does offer some good coping strategies for beating the cravings.

By m on 18 April 2016
Format: Kindle Edition Verified Purchase
Very helpful and motivational

My second book is a book of recipes for non-alcoholic drinks.

It is called, unsurprisingly: *"Alcohol Free Drinks – What to drink when you no longer drink"*!

Free download

www.threepeaspublishing.com/alcoholfreedrinks

I also got requests for a paperback version so I have now released a second edition through Amazon and the link is here:

https://www.amazon.co.uk/Alcohol-Drinks-drink-control-alcohol/dp/1530587735

What does the book cover? Well not drinking should open up your world but anxiety about what to drink at events or just on a romantic evening makes the early months of being sober stressful.

I tell the story in the book about coming up against a barman at an event who actually curled his lip at me when I asked for something non-alcoholic. He told me that he did not know what to serve. I said it was lucky that I had published a book and peered over the bar and told him what to mix with what.

Anyway, the book is written to inspire you if you want to control alcohol or be alcohol free for an evening, a day, a month or forever. This book will help you solve the problem and overcome the fear of – what on earth am I going to drink if I am not drinking or if I am cutting down? This book is aimed at everyone who wants to drink less and have a better life. Nowadays, that is a lot of us. You don't have to sign up to Alcoholics Anonymous or go into rehab to want to cut down or stop drinking temporarily or permanently. You just want a rest or to dial down the significance that alcohol has in your life. This book will help you see the changes you are making as positively delicious. This book will also help you to find great things to drink so you don't miss the alcohol.

I also talk a bit about whether to go for "low alcohol" drinks or avoid it all together in Chapter 1 but this is a book of recipes with no alcohol at all.

My aim was not to ape drinking alcohol but to provide an alternative set of ideas of what to drink. My view is that if you are not drinking or cutting down, it is better to get away from drinks that are taste-alikes or lookalikes because you risk feeling deprived.

These recipes are not about deprivation, they are about celebrating healthy living. You won't find any sack cloth and ashes punishment green gloop drinks here. In this book you will find recipes for example: Fresh & fruity: Spiced Apple Twister or Purple Passion. Warming & cooling: Hot Chocolate Love or Cold Orange. Intense Celebratory & comfy hot: Sparkling Cherry Spritzer or Banana Custard Toddy. That sounds pretty good, doesn't it?

The final book on being AF is a nutrition-specific book called

"Nutrition to Combat Alcohol Cravings"

So this book offers more nutritional advice and recipes. The recipes help you rebuild your body after the assault of alcohol. Second, they reduce your reliance on sugar. Sugar is a major contributor to cravings and relapse so managing your blood sugar is key. Sugar can also become an addiction to replace alcohol. The book also recommends long term nutritional goals.

• Long term nutritional goals to support your recovery

- Emergency nutrition plan to help you in early recovery
- Vitamins & Minerals
- The foods that help your body recover
- The drinks that help your body recover
- Recipes to support early recovery
- Breakfast, lunch, dinner, snacks
- Juicing for fast results.

The quick link is to the book on Amazon is here:

http://www.amazon.com/dp/B01BQ92X58

This has also has some nice reviews, which I reproduce here:

Recommended
By Cuéntame on 24 Mar. 2016
Format: Kindle Edition Verified Purchase
This is a very valuable book for anyone attempting to negotiate their way through early sobriety using nutrition as a support to help create strong foundations.
This book is particularly helpful with relation to the subject of cravings, which although mentioned in some books about recovery can also be glossed over somewhat. The implication is often that you're just supposed to resist them, but cravings can be frightening and undermine our confidence in our ability to live without alcohol.
I particularly like the practical nature of the book. Compact and clear. Lots of advice and some recipes offered but no overly extreme eating plan to follow. Rather you are nudged in the right direction towards giving your body the nutritional support it needs to repair the damage brought about by alcohol.
Catherine has been through all this herself and has poured her experience and passion for the alcohol free life into this book.

Highly recommended.
By Eugene Burndam on 7 April 2016
Format: Kindle Edition Verified Purchase
I really enjoyed the practicality of this guide and how the author explains the different alcoholic and post alcoholic disorders. There was a great linear approach to book's structure with understanding addiction and solving the problem with explaining different foods and then the practical application of having the reader create his or her own diet through recipes. This is a book to really help the reader take action with their addiction.

If you are interested in nutrition, fitness and wellness, you can subscribe to news, offers and How To videos on nutrition (including my books), nutrition and resilience via my publisher, Three Peas Publishing.

To subscribe, go to www.threepeaspublishing.com.

Three Peas Media also has a YouTube Channel "Three Peas Media" which provides videos on fitness and nutrition and resilience.

Finally, I would be very grateful if you would review this book for me when you are prompted to do so if you are reading this book on an ereader, or by visiting the book selling platform if you are reading this in paperback. I read all my reviews and I would also welcome any suggestions for other subjects you would like covered.

For ease, here is the Amazon link to review this book

http://www.amazon.com/dp/B01BNUX2P0

You can also reach me by email at hello@threepeaspublishing.com if you head your email FAO Maia Lloyd.

One last thing…

I really hope that you have enjoyed this book and have found some things which will help you take the first step or go forward confidently into the life you could lead if alcohol is not holding you back.

They say that you regret the things that you don't do rather than the things you do. Taking alcohol out of pole position is something, that if you don't do it, you will regret. Don't believe all the hype about it being an impossibility or being a miserable existence. It absolutely is not difficult or miserable.

If you approach being alcohol free using all the tools in this book and lots of other reading you can do on the benefits of being AF or moderate, if you use the nutrition advice, the research quoted in this book proves that you are 80% likely to succeed!

Just think what it would be like in a year's time to look back at your old time and know that you had said goodbye to the old you and actually got on with the one thing that would make the most difference to your life. That is barely a fantasy because it is so do-able.

I wrote this book because I could not find much practical, real life advice for people in the early stages of the exciting journey of recovery. There were lots of books which were personal accounts of the worst of times but not much from a coaching mindset, a "you can do it!" mindset, which is what I wanted. I wanted a cheerleader not a commiserator.

So, I wrote this book. I hope it has been inspirational and confidence boosting.

If you liked this book and found it useful, I would be really grateful if you could post a short review on Amazon. Your support really does make a difference and I read all reviews personally so I can get feedback and make this book even better. The Amazon link for this book where you can leave a review is

www.amazon.com/dp/B01BNUX2P0

Thanks again for your support

Catherine Mason Thomas

You can reach me if you have comments or suggestions for what else would be help for me to cover at hello@threepeaspublishing.com. Just mark the email FAO Catherine Mason Thomas

Good Luck.

Made in the USA
Middletown, DE
31 August 2016